GRAPHIC LIBRARY™

GRAPHIC BIOGRAPHIES

SAMUEL ADAMS

PATRIOT AND STATESMAN

by Matt Doeden

illustrated by Tod Smith, Keith Wilson,
Dave Hoover, and Charles Barnett III

Consultant:
Wayne Bodle
Assistant Professor of History
Indiana University of Pennsylvania

Capstone
press®

Mankato, Minnesota

Graphic Library is published by Capstone Press,
151 Good Counsel Drive, P.O. Box 669, Mankato, Minnesota 56002.
www.capstonepress.com

Printed in the United States of America

1 2 3 4 5 6 11 10 09 08 07 06

Library of Congress Cataloging-in-Publication Data
Doeden, Matt.
Samuel Adams : patriot and statesman / by Matt Doeden; illustrated by Tod Smith, Keith Wilson, Dave Hoover, and Charles Barnett III.
p. cm.—(Graphic library. Graphic biographies)
Includes bibliographical references and index.
ISBN-13: 978-0-7368-6500-5 (hardcover)
ISBN-10: 0-7368-6500-4 (hardcover)
ISBN-13: 978-0-7368-9664-1 (softcover pbk.)
ISBN-10: 0-7368-9664-3 (softcover pbk.)
1. Adams, Samuel, 1722–1803—Juvenile literature. 2. Politicians—United States—Biography—Juvenile literature. 3. United States. Declaration of Independence—Signers—Biography—Juvenile literature. 4. United States—History—Revolution, 1775–1783—Biography—Juvenile literature. I. Title. II. Series.
E302.6.A2D64 2007
973.3092—dc22 2006004845

Summary: In graphic novel format, tells the life story of American patriot Samuel Adams and his role in the events that led to the Revolutionary War.

Designer
Bob Lentz

Production Artists
Scott Thoms and Kim Brown

Colorist
Matt Hennen

Editor
Erika L. Shores

Editor's note: Direct quotations from primary sources are indicated by a yellow background.

Direct quotations appear on the following pages:
Page 5, from *Two Treatises of Government* by John Locke (London: A. and J. Churchill, 1694).
Page 13, from *The Writings of Samuel Adams, collected and edited by Harry Alonzo Cushing* by Samuel Adams (New York: Octagon Books, 1968).
Page 16, from *Samuel Adams* by James K. Hosmer (New York: Houghton Mifflin, 1899).

TABLE OF CONTENTS

Chapter 1
Born in Boston

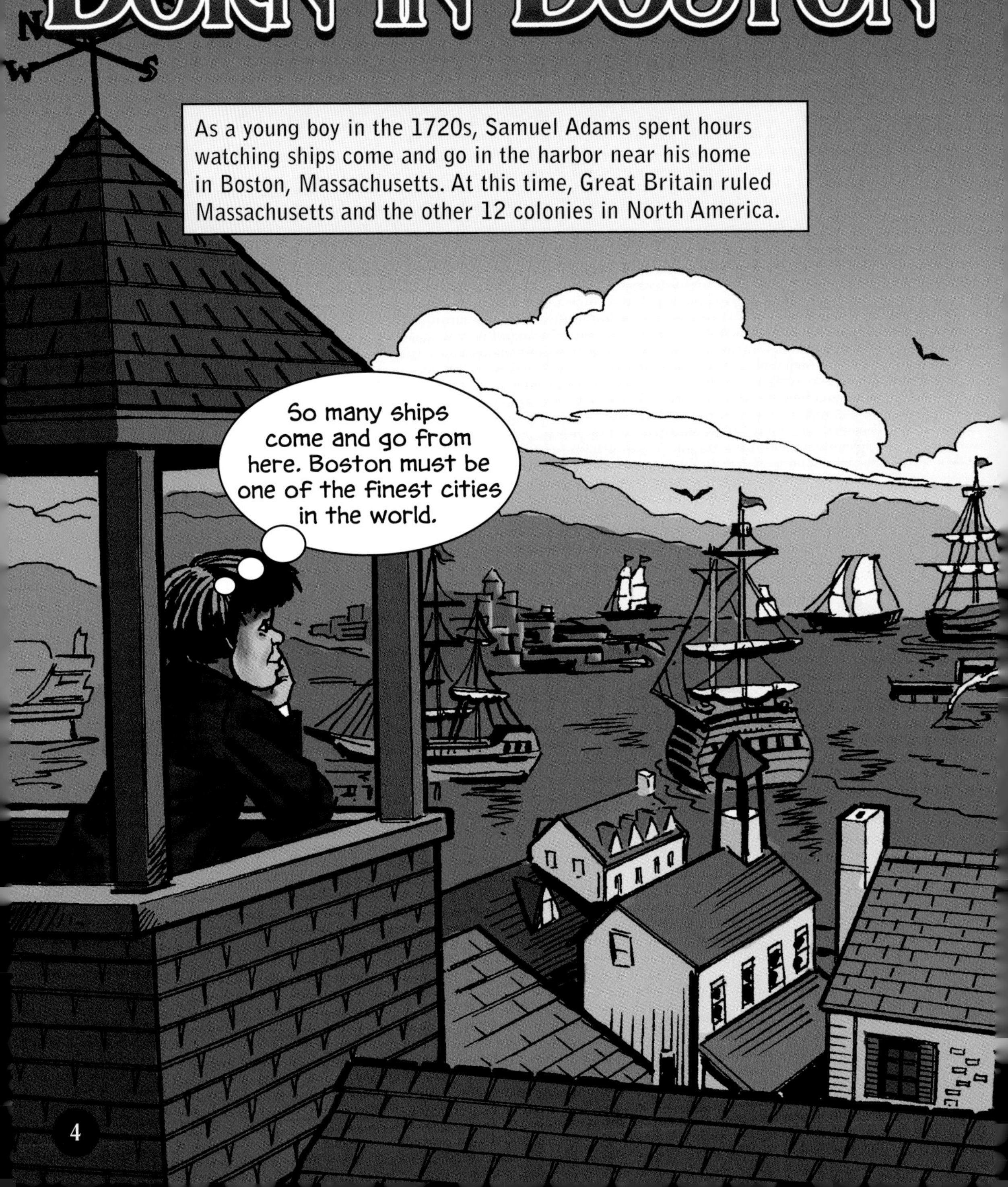
N
W
S
As a young boy in the 1720s, Samuel Adams spent hours watching ships come and go in the harbor near his home in Boston, Massachusetts. At this time, Great Britain ruled Massachusetts and the other 12 colonies in North America.
So many ships come and go from here. Boston must be one of the finest cities in the world.

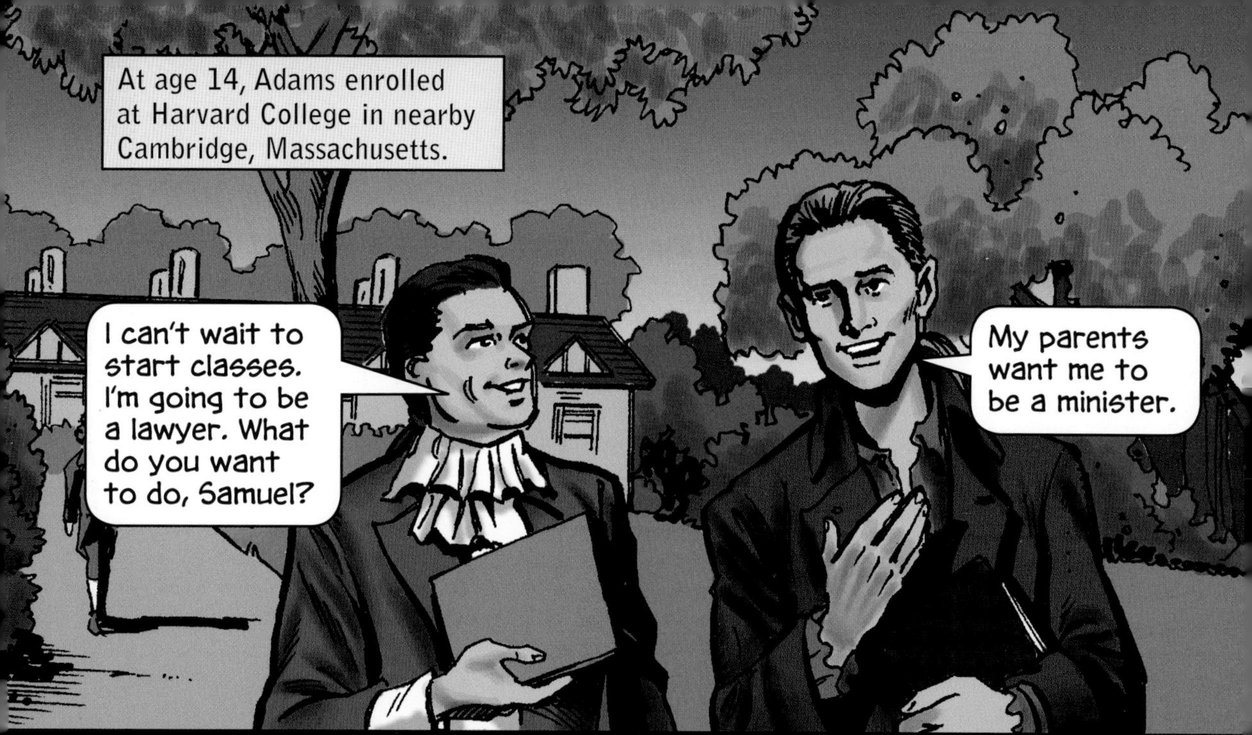
At age 14, Adams enrolled at Harvard College in nearby Cambridge, Massachusetts.
I can't wait to start classes. I'm going to be a lawyer. What do you want to do, Samuel?
My parents want me to be a minister.

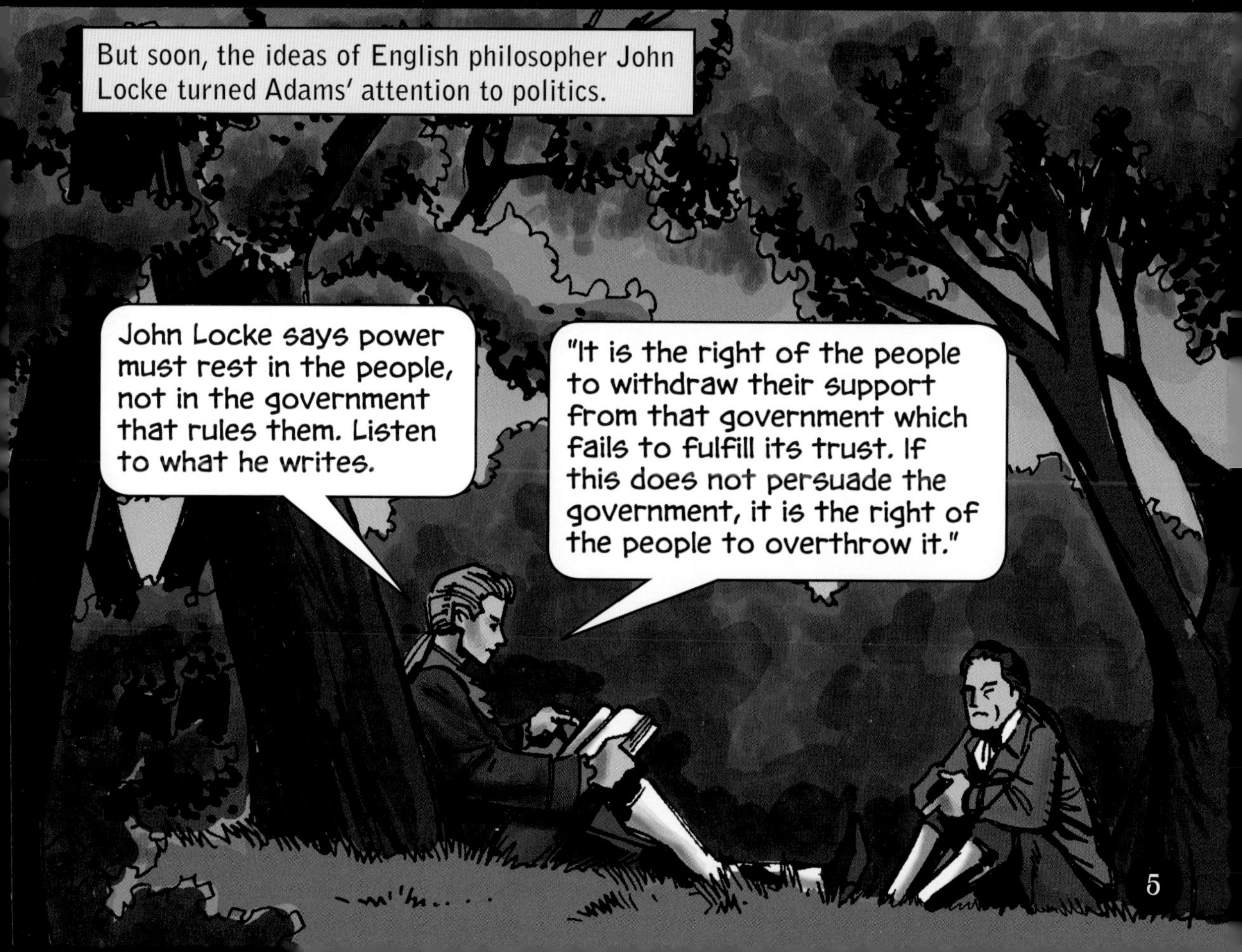
But soon, the ideas of English philosopher John Locke turned Adams' attention to politics.
John Locke says power must rest in the people, not in the government that rules them. Listen to what he writes.
"It is the right of the people to withdraw their support from that government which fails to fulfill its trust. If this does not persuade the government, it is the right of the people to overthrow it."

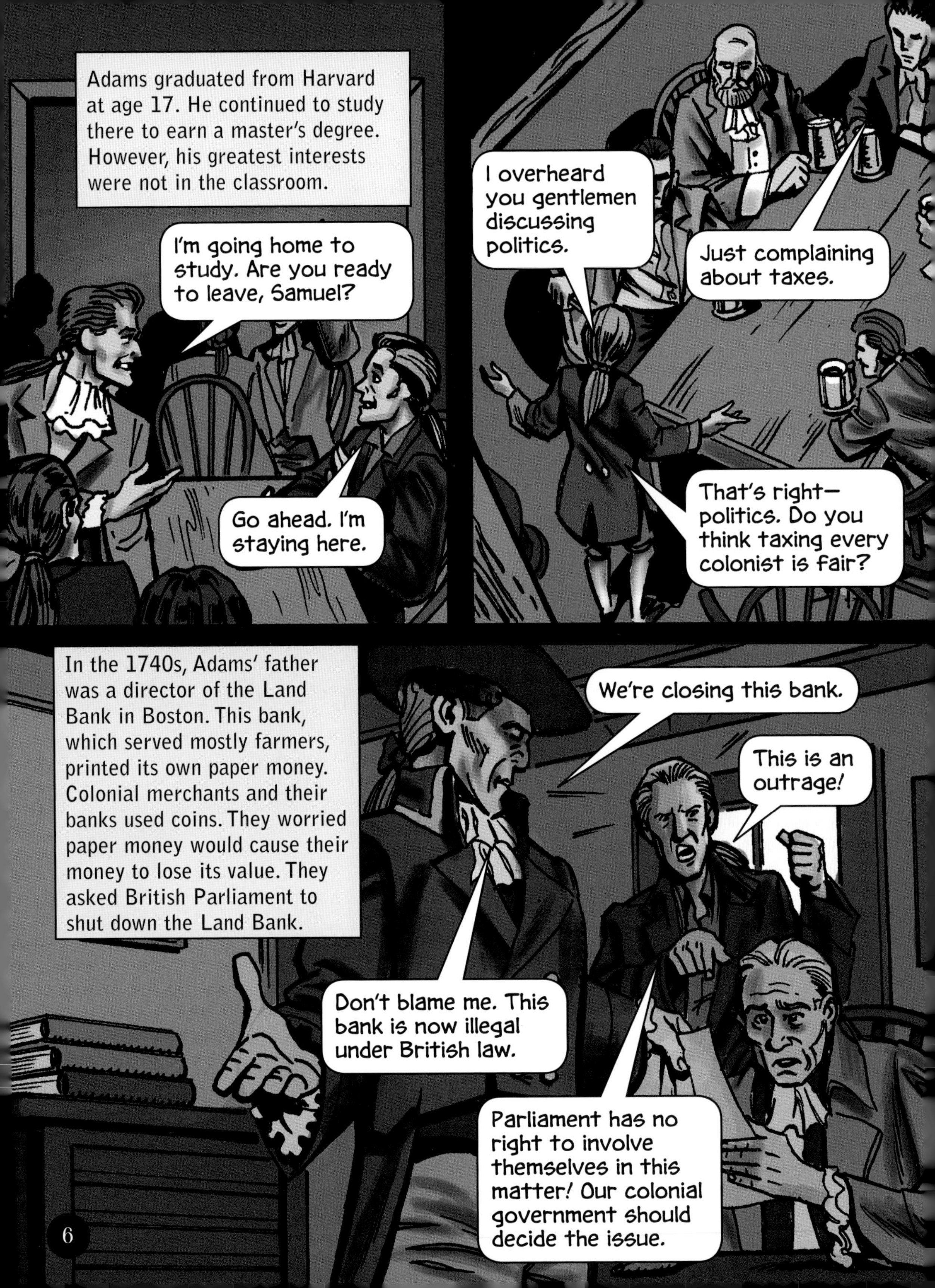
Adams graduated from Harvard at age 17. He continued to study there to earn a master's degree. However, his greatest interests were not in the classroom.
I'm going home to study. Are you ready to leave, Samuel?
Go ahead. I'm staying here.
I overheard you gentlemen discussing politics.
Just complaining about taxes.
That's right—politics. Do you think taxing every colonist is fair?
In the 1740s, Adams' father was a director of the Land Bank in Boston. This bank, which served mostly farmers, printed its own paper money. Colonial merchants and their banks used coins. They worried paper money would cause their money to lose its value. They asked British Parliament to shut down the Land Bank.
We're closing this bank.
This is an outrage!
Don't blame me. This bank is now illegal under British law.
Parliament has no right to involve themselves in this matter! Our colonial government should decide the issue.

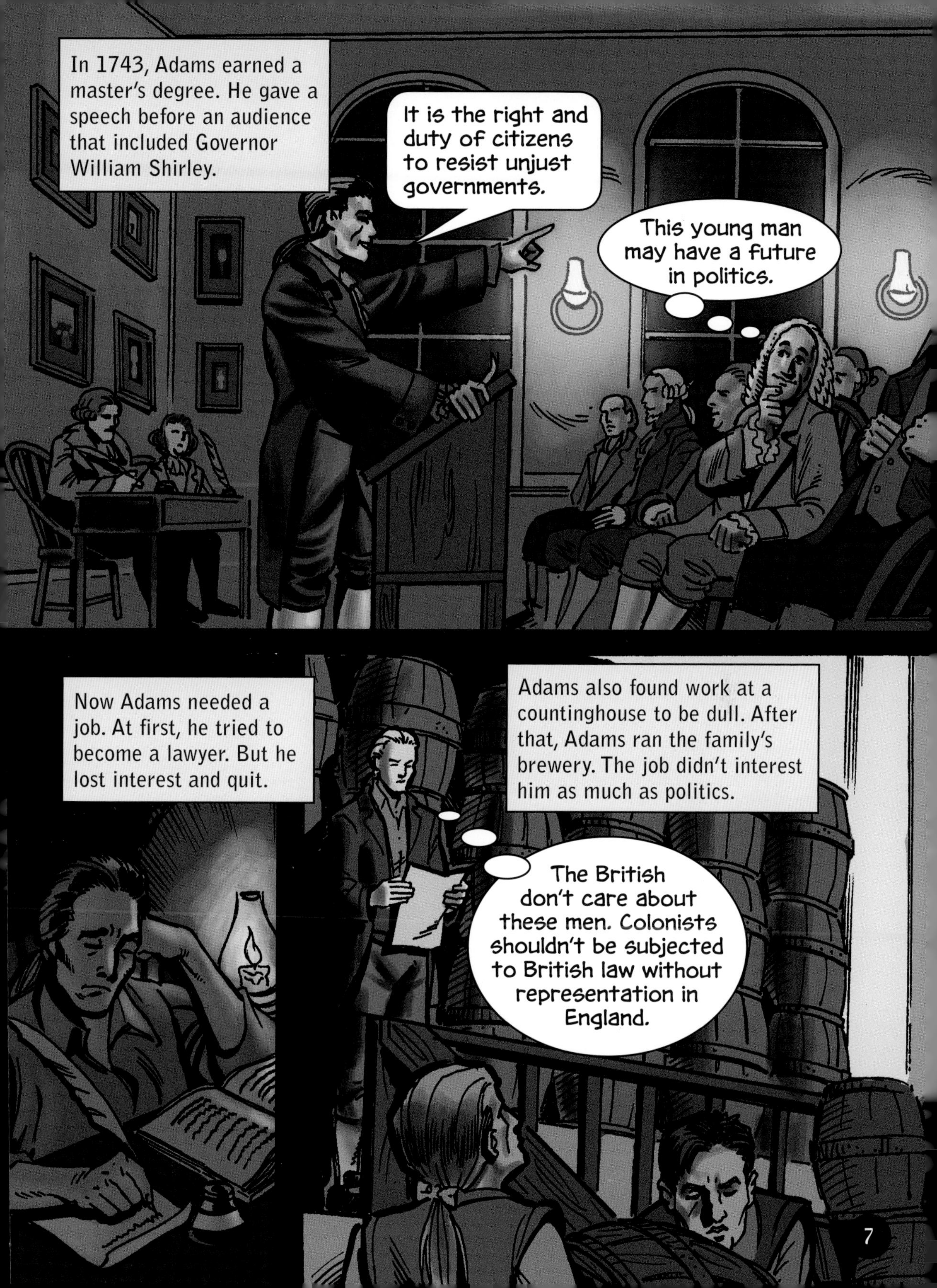
In 1743, Adams earned a master's degree. He gave a speech before an audience that included Governor William Shirley.
It is the right and duty of citizens to resist unjust governments.
This young man may have a future in politics.
Now Adams needed a job. At first, he tried to become a lawyer. But he lost interest and quit.
Adams also found work at a countinghouse to be dull. After that, Adams ran the family's brewery. The job didn't interest him as much as politics.
The British don't care about these men. Colonists shouldn't be subjected to British law without representation in England.

Chapter 2
Son of Liberty

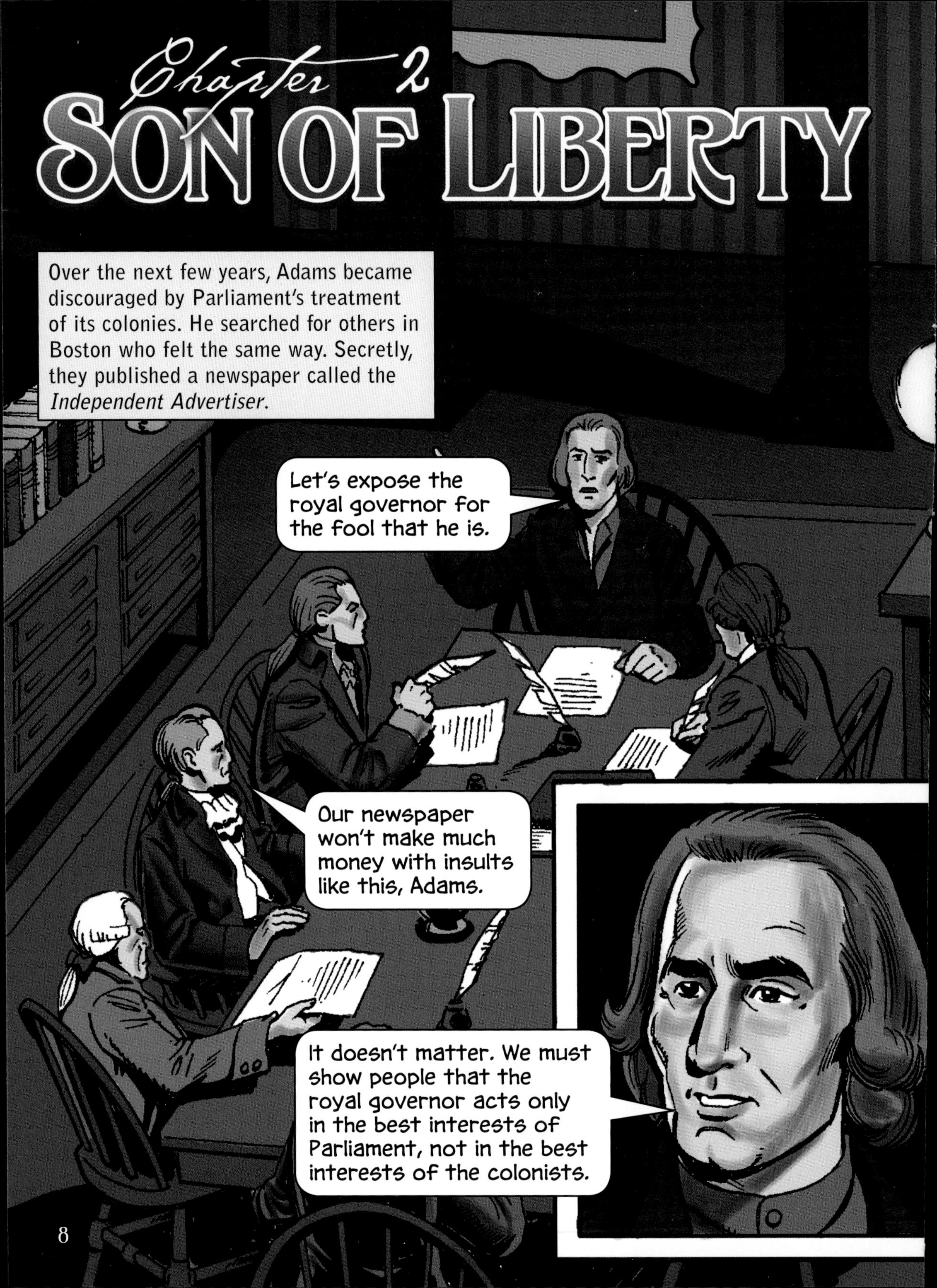

Over the next few years, Adams became discouraged by Parliament's treatment of its colonies. He searched for others in Boston who felt the same way. Secretly, they published a newspaper called the *Independent Advertiser*.
Let's expose the royal governor for the fool that he is.
Our newspaper won't make much money with insults like this, Adams.
It doesn't matter. We must show people that the royal governor acts only in the best interests of Parliament, not in the best interests of the colonists.

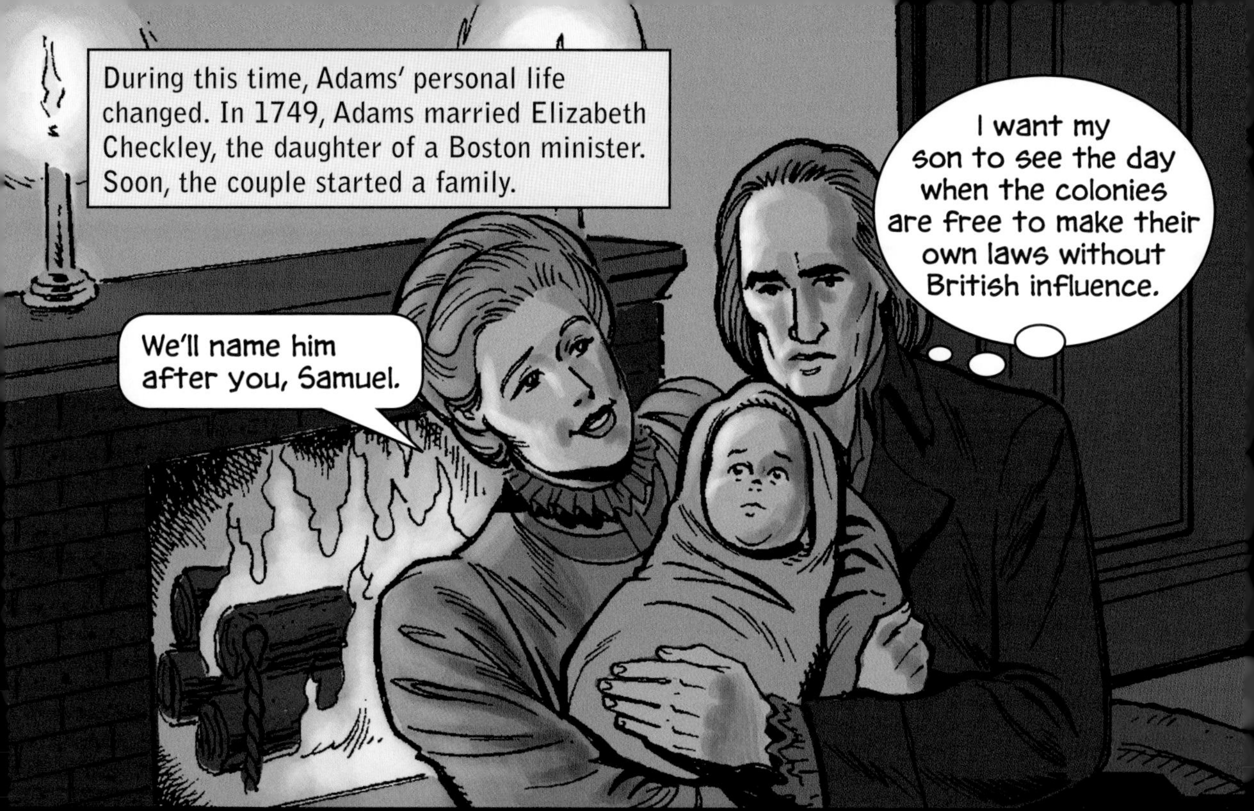
During this time, Adams' personal life changed. In 1749, Adams married Elizabeth Checkley, the daughter of a Boston minister. Soon, the couple started a family.
We'll name him after you, Samuel.
I want my son to see the day when the colonies are free to make their own laws without British influence.

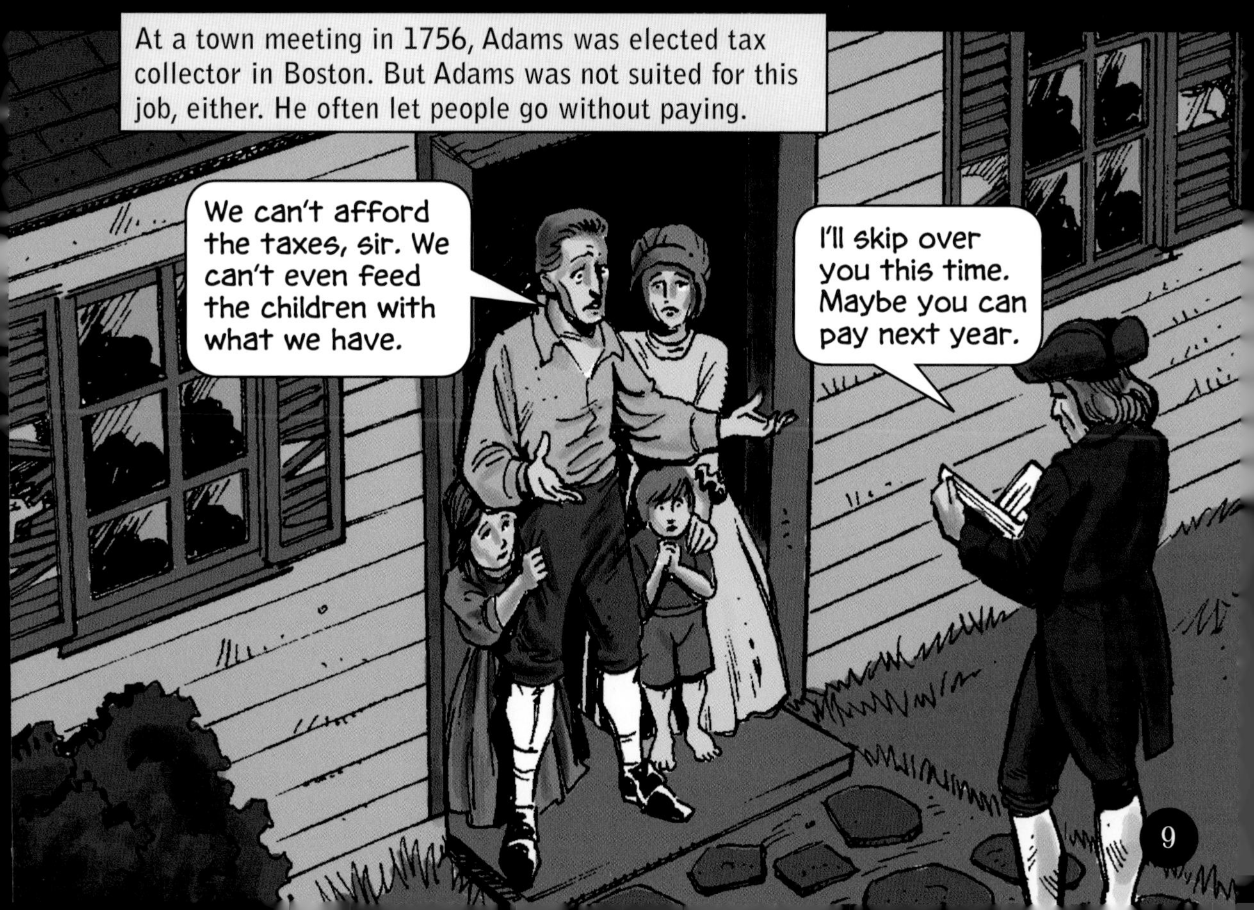
At a town meeting in 1756, Adams was elected tax collector in Boston. But Adams was not suited for this job, either. He often let people go without paying.
We can't afford the taxes, sir. We can't even feed the children with what we have.
I'll skip over you this time. Maybe you can pay next year.

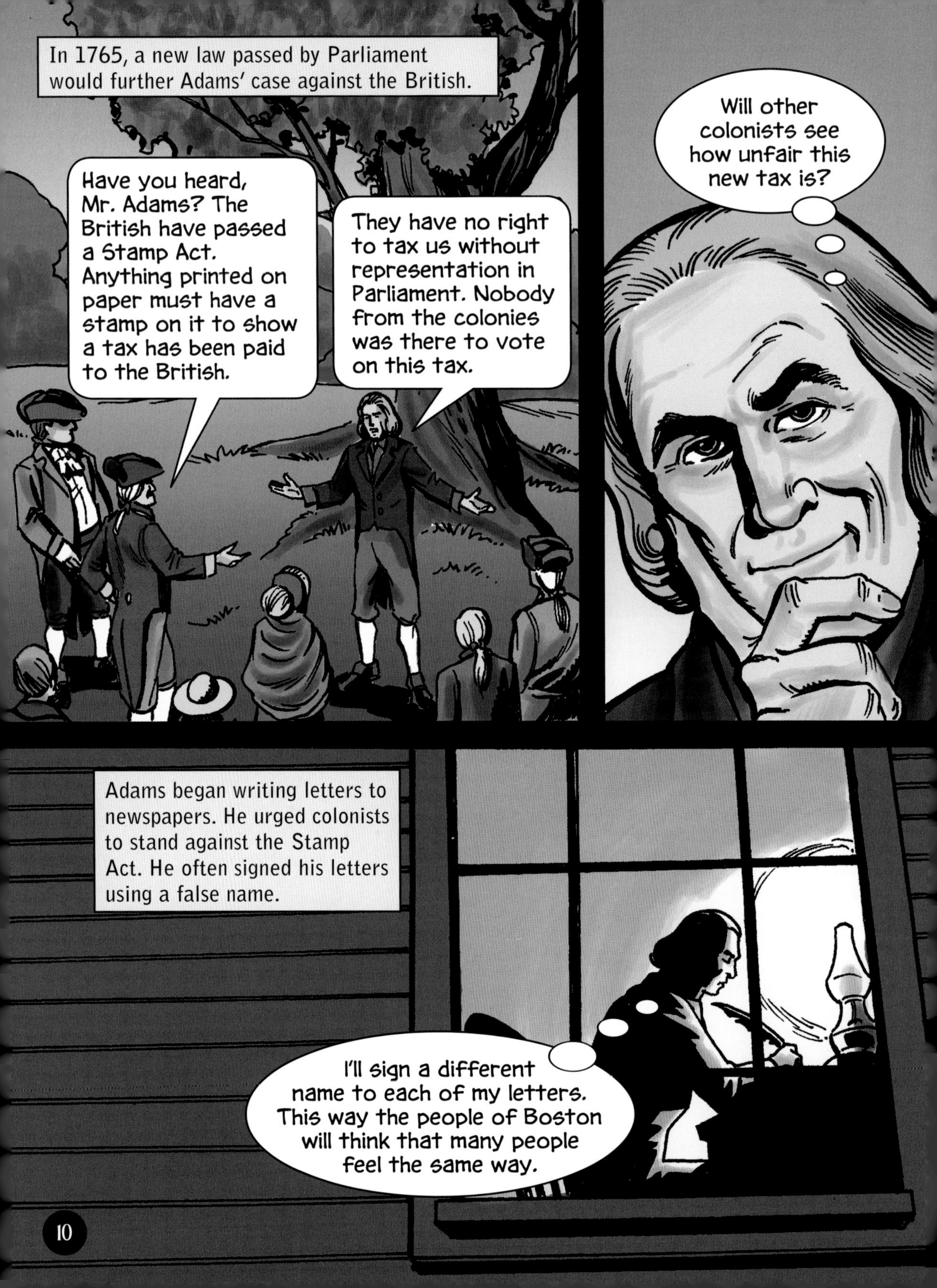
In 1765, a new law passed by Parliament would further Adams' case against the British.
Have you heard, Mr. Adams? The British have passed a Stamp Act. Anything printed on paper must have a stamp on it to show a tax has been paid to the British.
They have no right to tax us without representation in Parliament. Nobody from the colonies was there to vote on this tax.
Will other colonists see how unfair this new tax is?
Adams began writing letters to newspapers. He urged colonists to stand against the Stamp Act. He often signed his letters using a false name.
I'll sign a different name to each of my letters. This way the people of Boston will think that many people feel the same way.

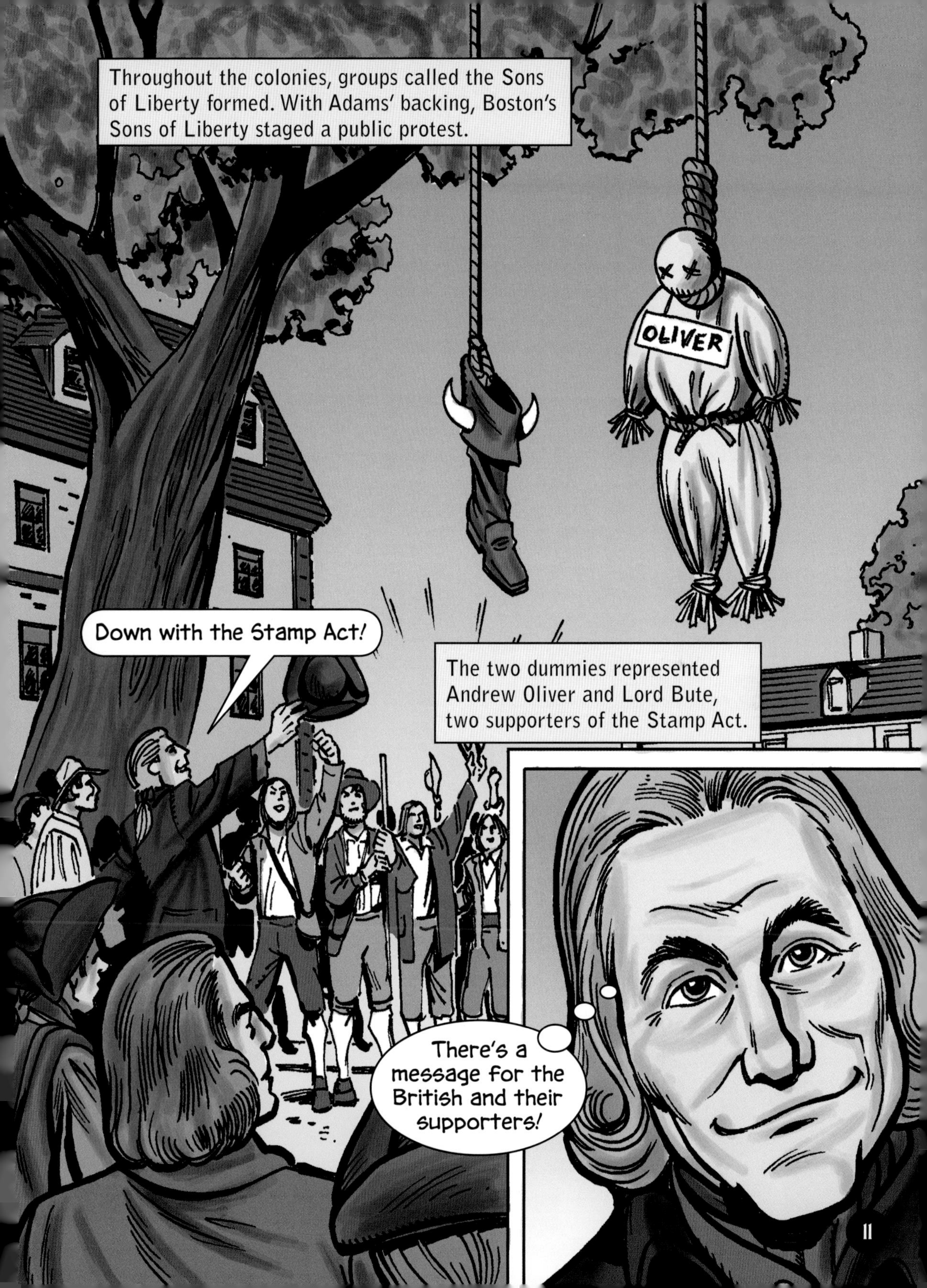
Throughout the colonies, groups called the Sons of Liberty formed. With Adams' backing, Boston's Sons of Liberty staged a public protest.
OLIVER
Down with the Stamp Act!
The two dummies represented Andrew Oliver and Lord Bute, two supporters of the Stamp Act.
There's a message for the British and their supporters!

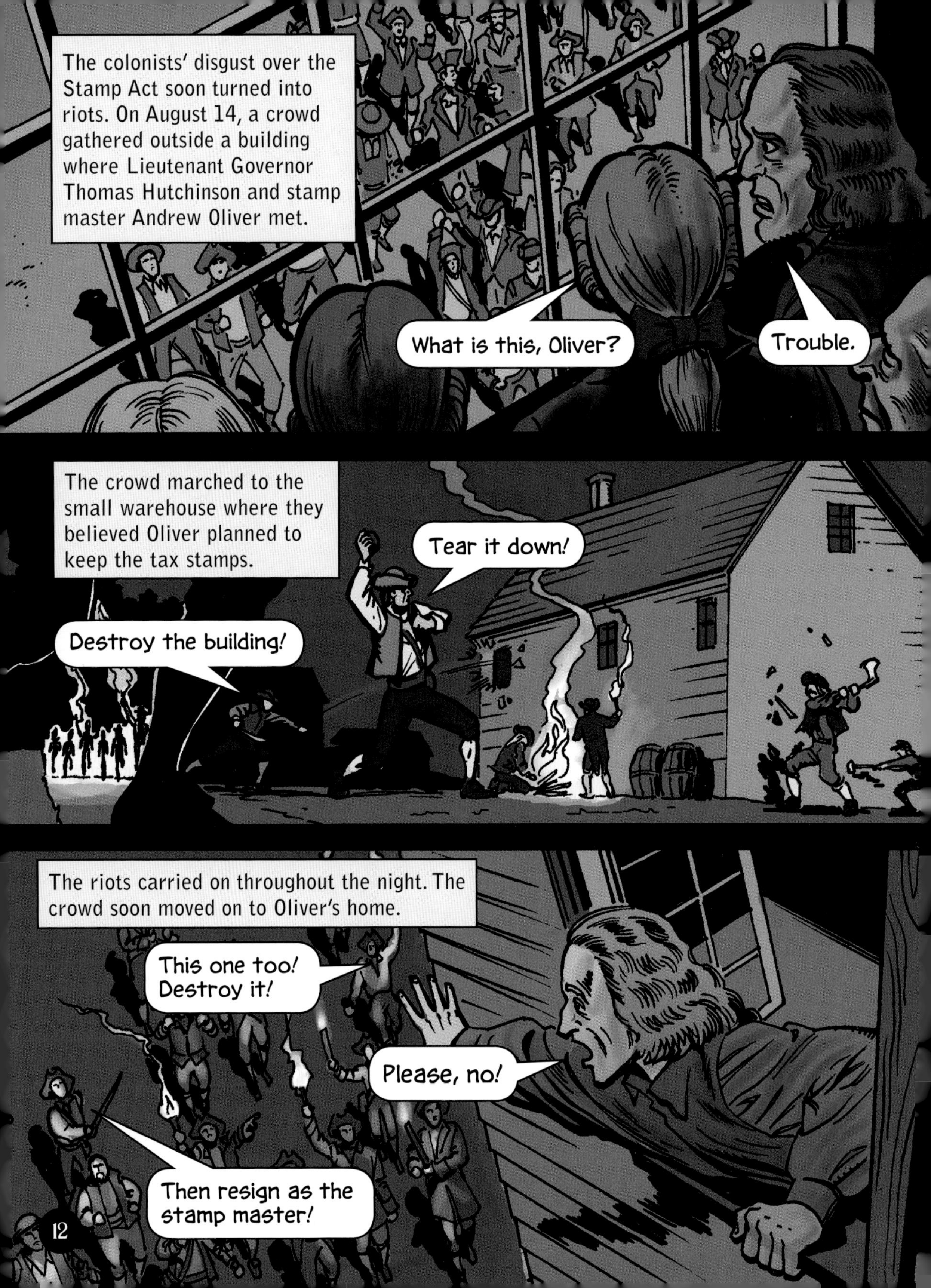
The colonists' disgust over the Stamp Act soon turned into riots. On August 14, a crowd gathered outside a building where Lieutenant Governor Thomas Hutchinson and stamp master Andrew Oliver met.
What is this, Oliver?
Trouble.
The crowd marched to the small warehouse where they believed Oliver planned to keep the tax stamps.
Tear it down!
Destroy the building!
The riots carried on throughout the night. The crowd soon moved on to Oliver's home.
This one too! Destroy it!
Please, no!
Then resign as the stamp master!

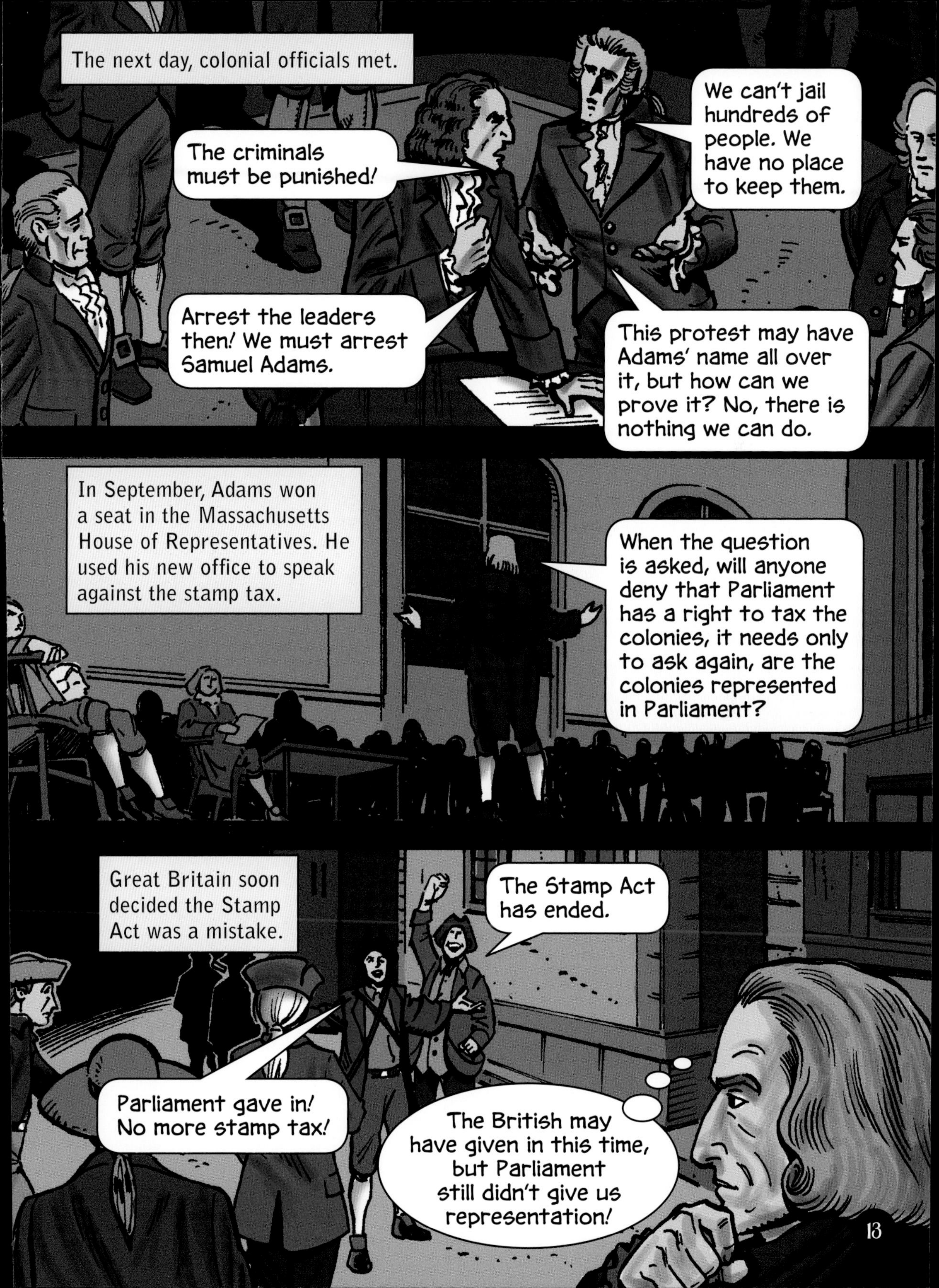

The next day, colonial officials met.
The criminals must be punished!
We can't jail hundreds of people. We have no place to keep them.
Arrest the leaders then! We must arrest Samuel Adams.
This protest may have Adams' name all over it, but how can we prove it? No, there is nothing we can do.
In September, Adams won a seat in the Massachusetts House of Representatives. He used his new office to speak against the stamp tax.
When the question is asked, will anyone deny that Parliament has a right to tax the colonies, it needs only to ask again, are the colonies represented in Parliament?
Great Britain soon decided the Stamp Act was a mistake.
The Stamp Act has ended.
Parliament gave in! No more stamp tax!
The British may have given in this time, but Parliament still didn't give us representation!

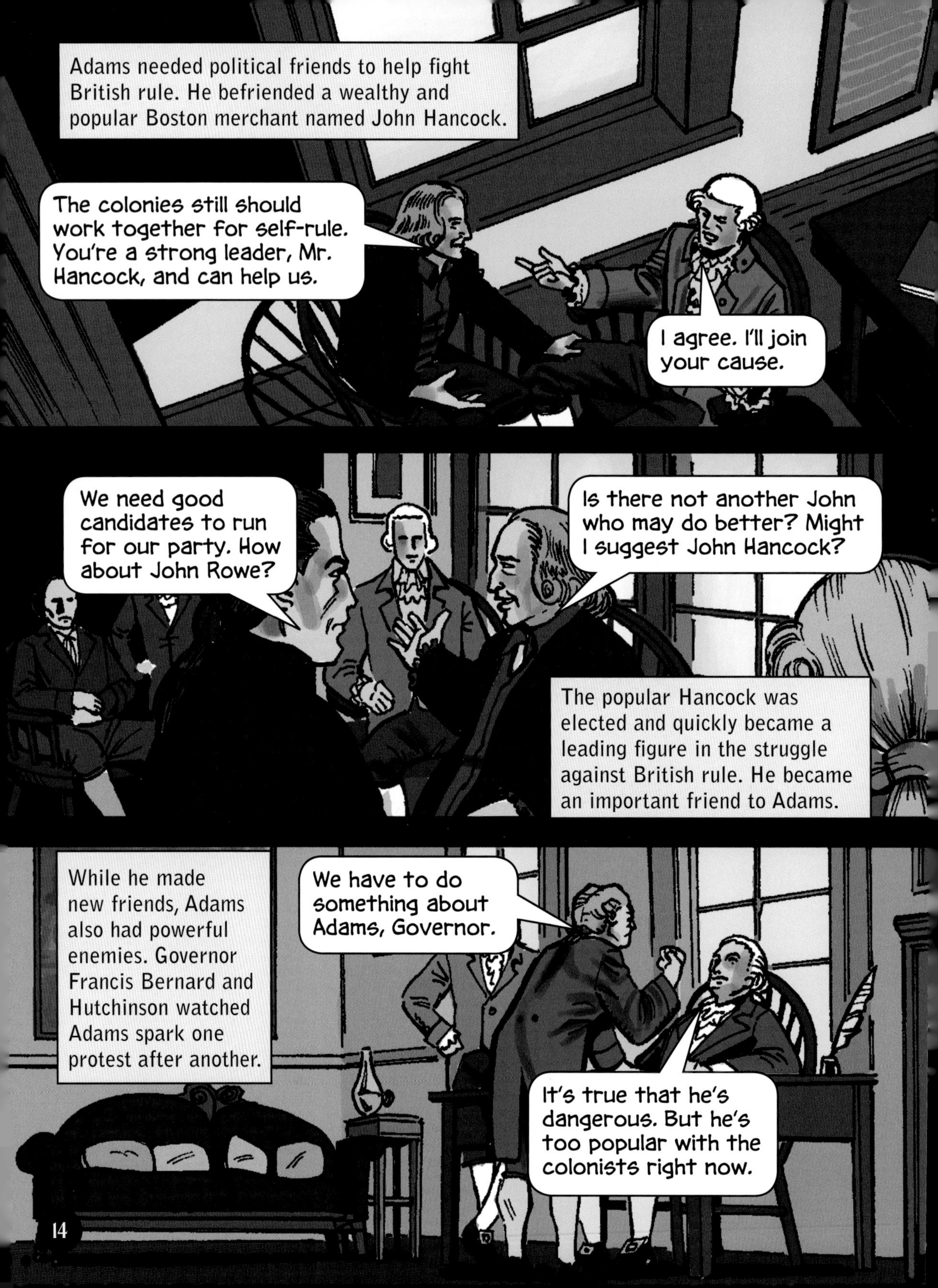
Adams needed political friends to help fight British rule. He befriended a wealthy and popular Boston merchant named John Hancock.
The colonies still should work together for self-rule. You're a strong leader, Mr. Hancock, and can help us.
I agree. I'll join your cause.
We need good candidates to run for our party. How about John Rowe?
Is there not another John who may do better? Might I suggest John Hancock?
The popular Hancock was elected and quickly became a leading figure in the struggle against British rule. He became an important friend to Adams.
While he made new friends, Adams also had powerful enemies. Governor Francis Bernard and Hutchinson watched Adams spark one protest after another.
We have to do something about Adams, Governor.
It's true that he's dangerous. But he's too popular with the colonists right now.

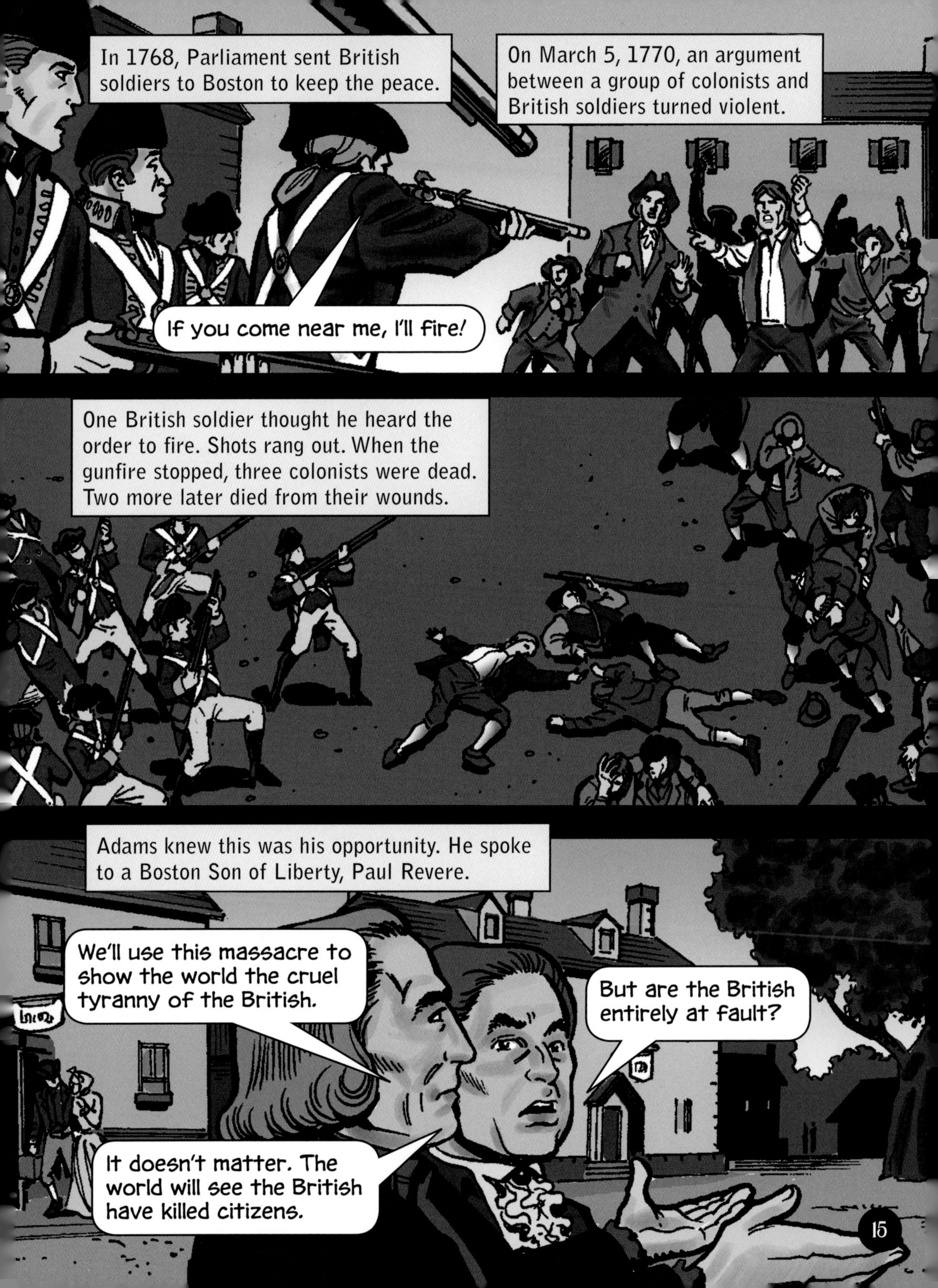
In 1768, Parliament sent British soldiers to Boston to keep the peace.
On March 5, 1770, an argument between a group of colonists and British soldiers turned violent.
If you come near me, I'll fire!
One British soldier thought he heard the order to fire. Shots rang out. When the gunfire stopped, three colonists were dead. Two more later died from their wounds.
Adams knew this was his opportunity. He spoke to a Boston Son of Liberty, Paul Revere.
We'll use this massacre to show the world the cruel tyranny of the British.
But are the British entirely at fault?
It doesn't matter. The world will see the British have killed citizens.

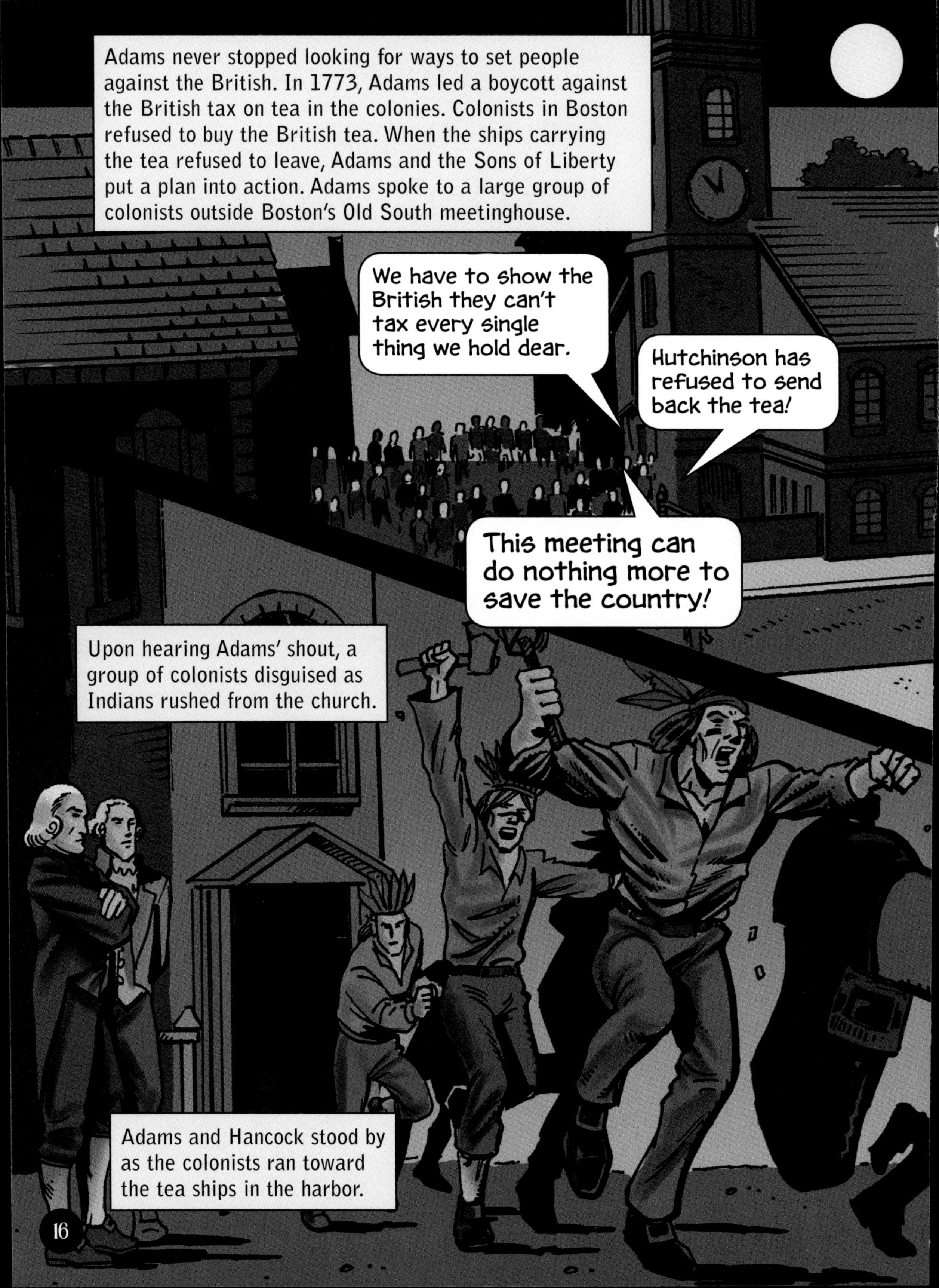
Adams never stopped looking for ways to set people against the British. In 1773, Adams led a boycott against the British tax on tea in the colonies. Colonists in Boston refused to buy the British tea. When the ships carrying the tea refused to leave, Adams and the Sons of Liberty put a plan into action. Adams spoke to a large group of colonists outside Boston's Old South meetinghouse.
We have to show the British they can't tax every single thing we hold dear.
Hutchinson has refused to send back the tea!
This meeting can do nothing more to save the country!
Upon hearing Adams' shout, a group of colonists disguised as Indians rushed from the church.
Adams and Hancock stood by as the colonists ran toward the tea ships in the harbor.

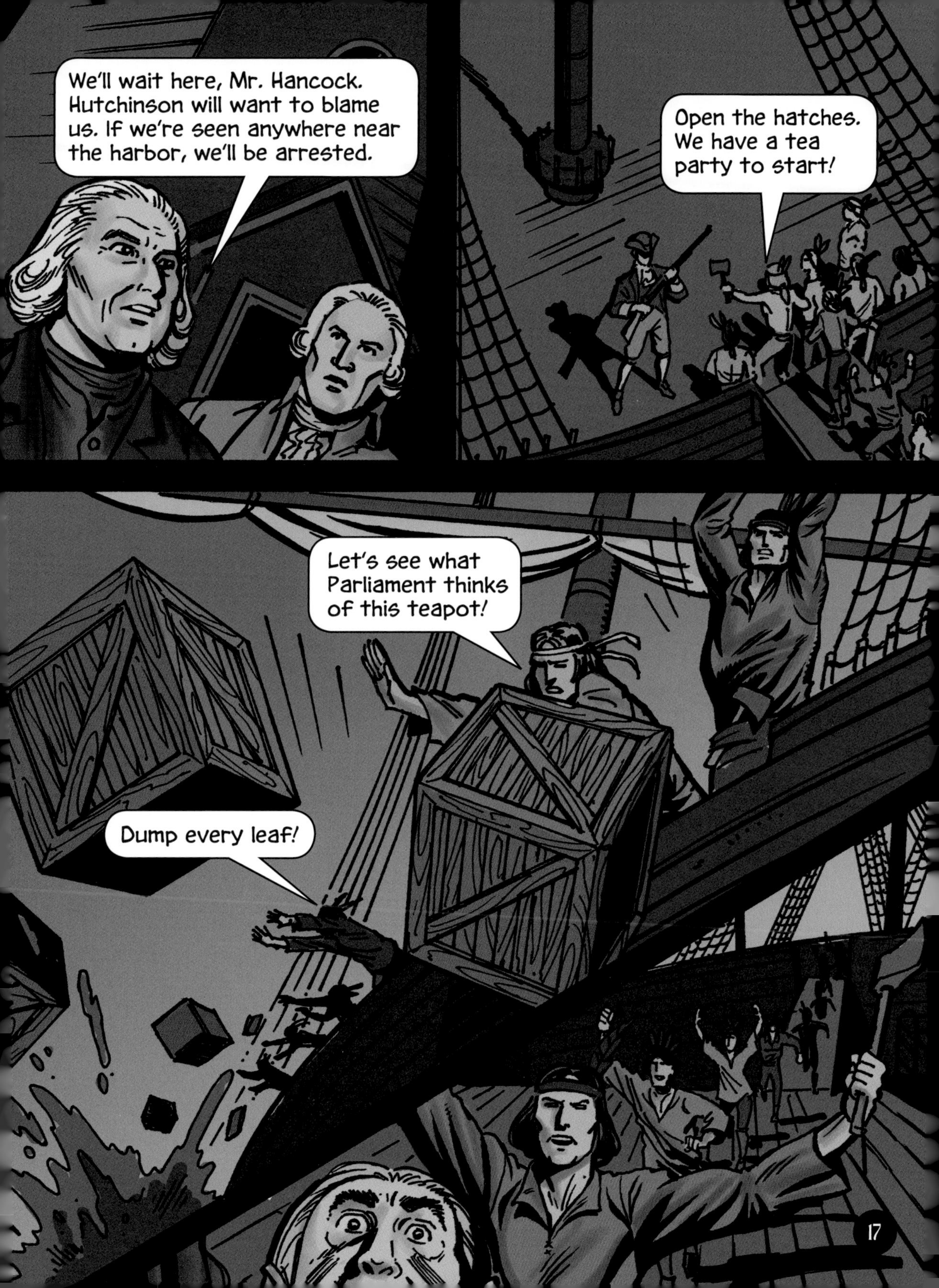
We'll wait here, Mr. Hancock. Hutchinson will want to blame us. If we're seen anywhere near the harbor, we'll be arrested.
Open the hatches. We have a tea party to start!
Let's see what Parliament thinks of this teapot!
Dump every leaf!

Chapter 3
The Revolution Begins

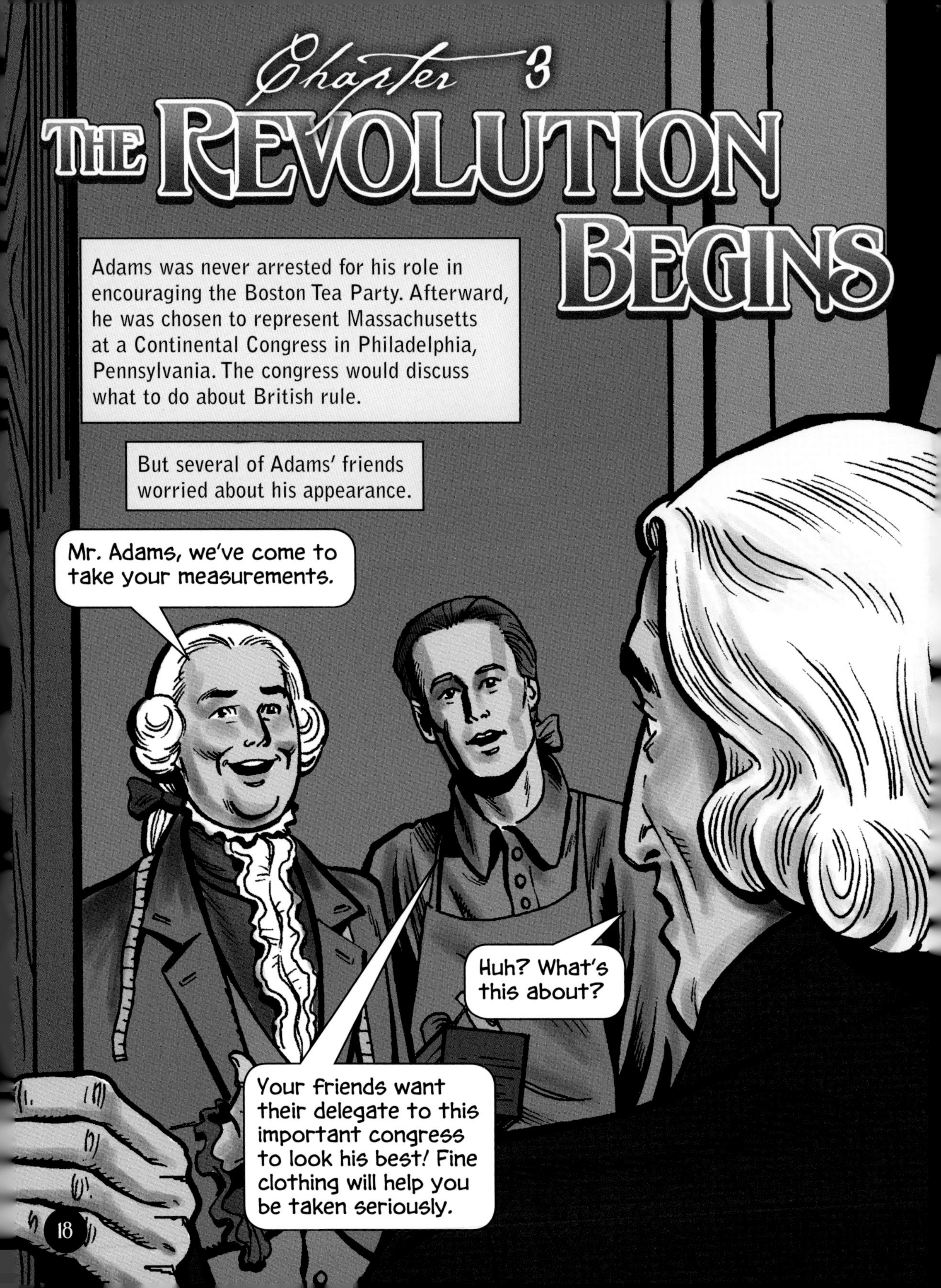
Adams was never arrested for his role in encouraging the Boston Tea Party. Afterward, he was chosen to represent Massachusetts at a Continental Congress in Philadelphia, Pennsylvania. The congress would discuss what to do about British rule.
But several of Adams' friends worried about his appearance.
Mr. Adams, we've come to take your measurements.
Huh? What's this about?
Your friends want their delegate to this important congress to look his best! Fine clothing will help you be taken seriously.

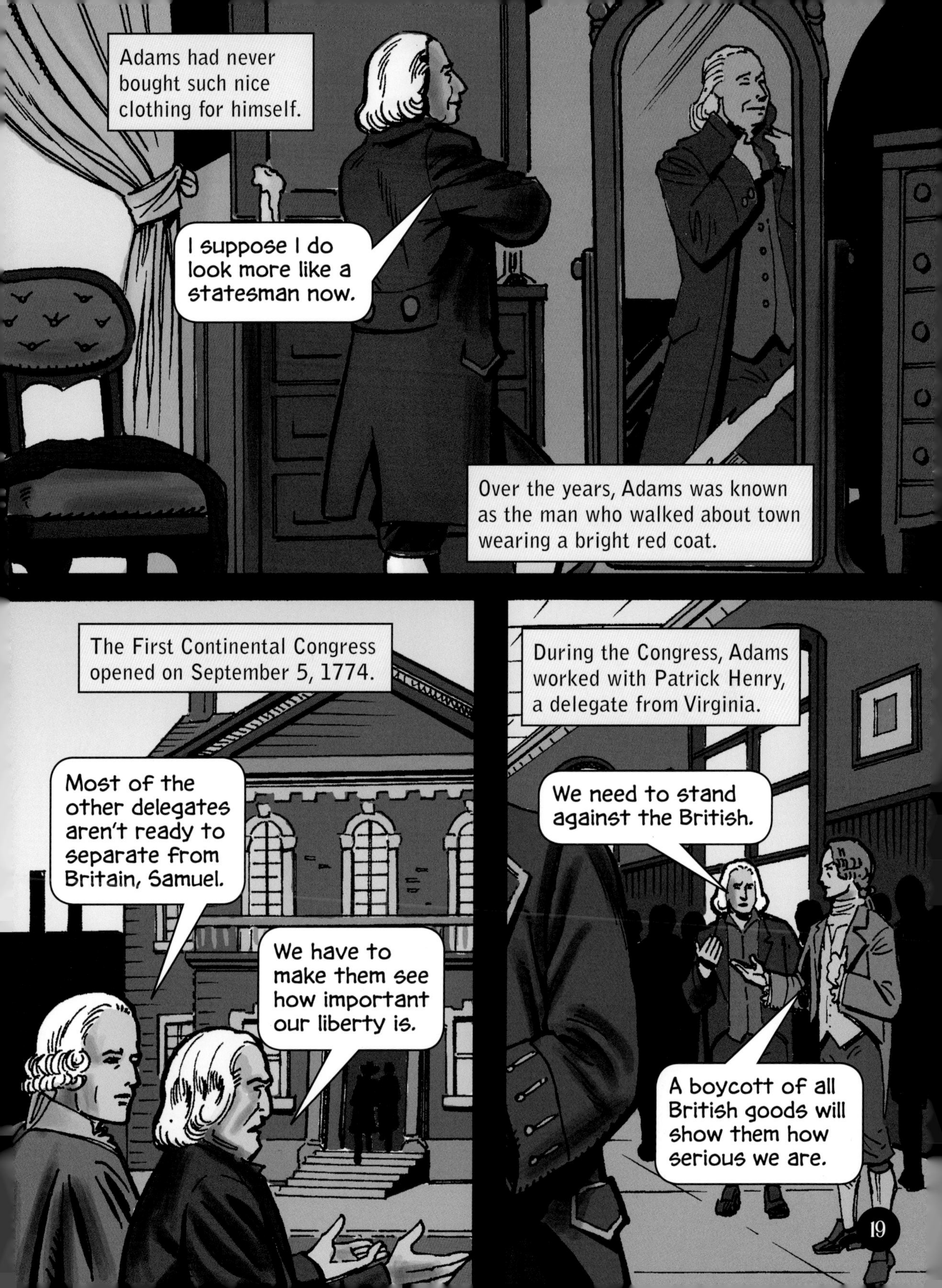
Adams had never bought such nice clothing for himself.
I suppose I do look more like a statesman now.
Over the years, Adams was known as the man who walked about town wearing a bright red coat.
The First Continental Congress opened on September 5, 1774.
Most of the other delegates aren't ready to separate from Britain, Samuel.
We have to make them see how important our liberty is.
During the Congress, Adams worked with Patrick Henry, a delegate from Virginia.
We need to stand against the British.
A boycott of all British goods will show them how serious we are.

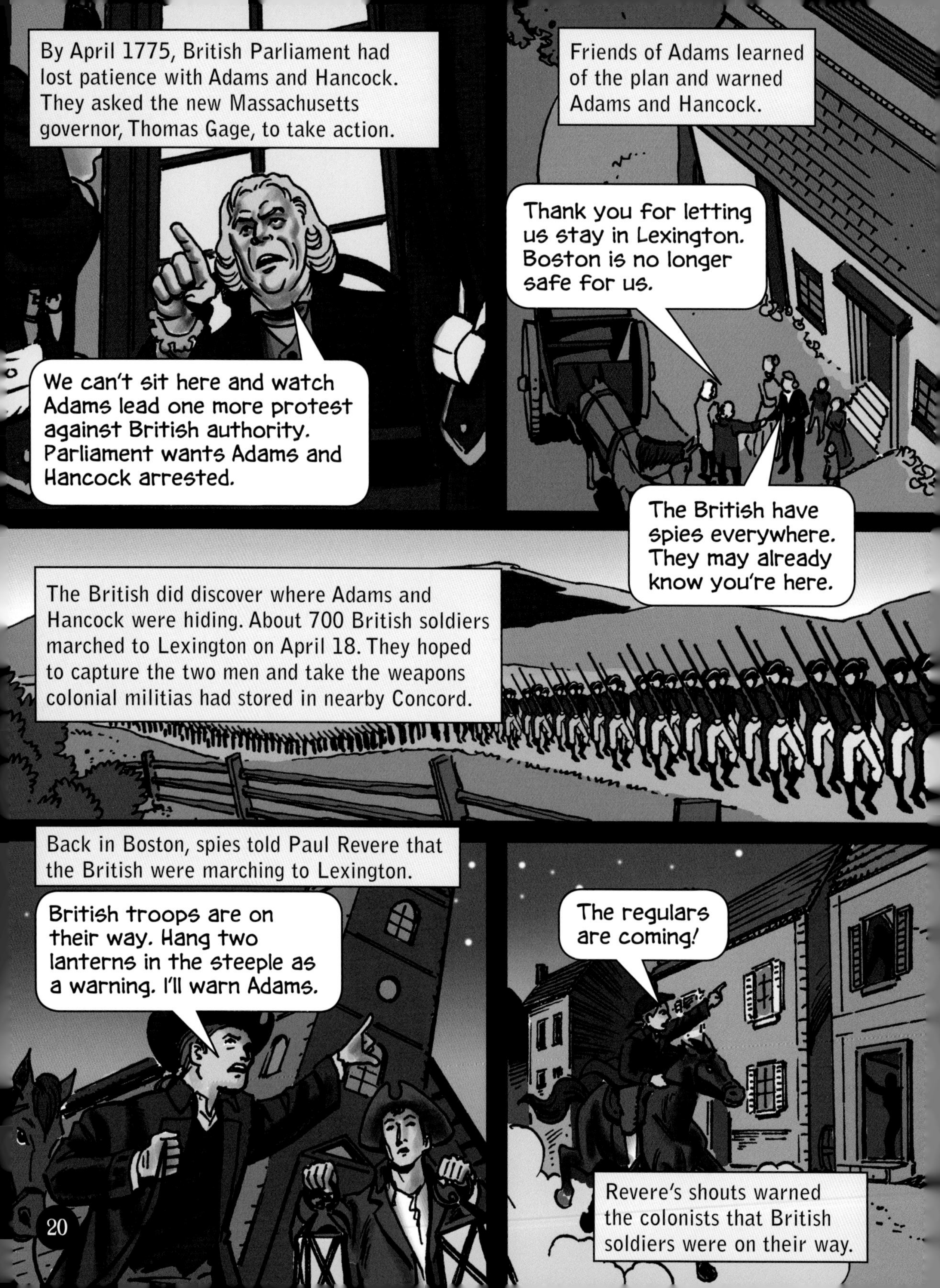
By April 1775, British Parliament had lost patience with Adams and Hancock. They asked the new Massachusetts governor, Thomas Gage, to take action.
We can't sit here and watch Adams lead one more protest against British authority. Parliament wants Adams and Hancock arrested.
Friends of Adams learned of the plan and warned Adams and Hancock.
Thank you for letting us stay in Lexington. Boston is no longer safe for us.
The British have spies everywhere. They may already know you're here.
The British did discover where Adams and Hancock were hiding. About 700 British soldiers marched to Lexington on April 18. They hoped to capture the two men and take the weapons colonial militias had stored in nearby Concord.
Back in Boston, spies told Paul Revere that the British were marching to Lexington.
British troops are on their way. Hang two lanterns in the steeple as a warning. I'll warn Adams.
The regulars are coming!
Revere's shouts warned the colonists that British soldiers were on their way.

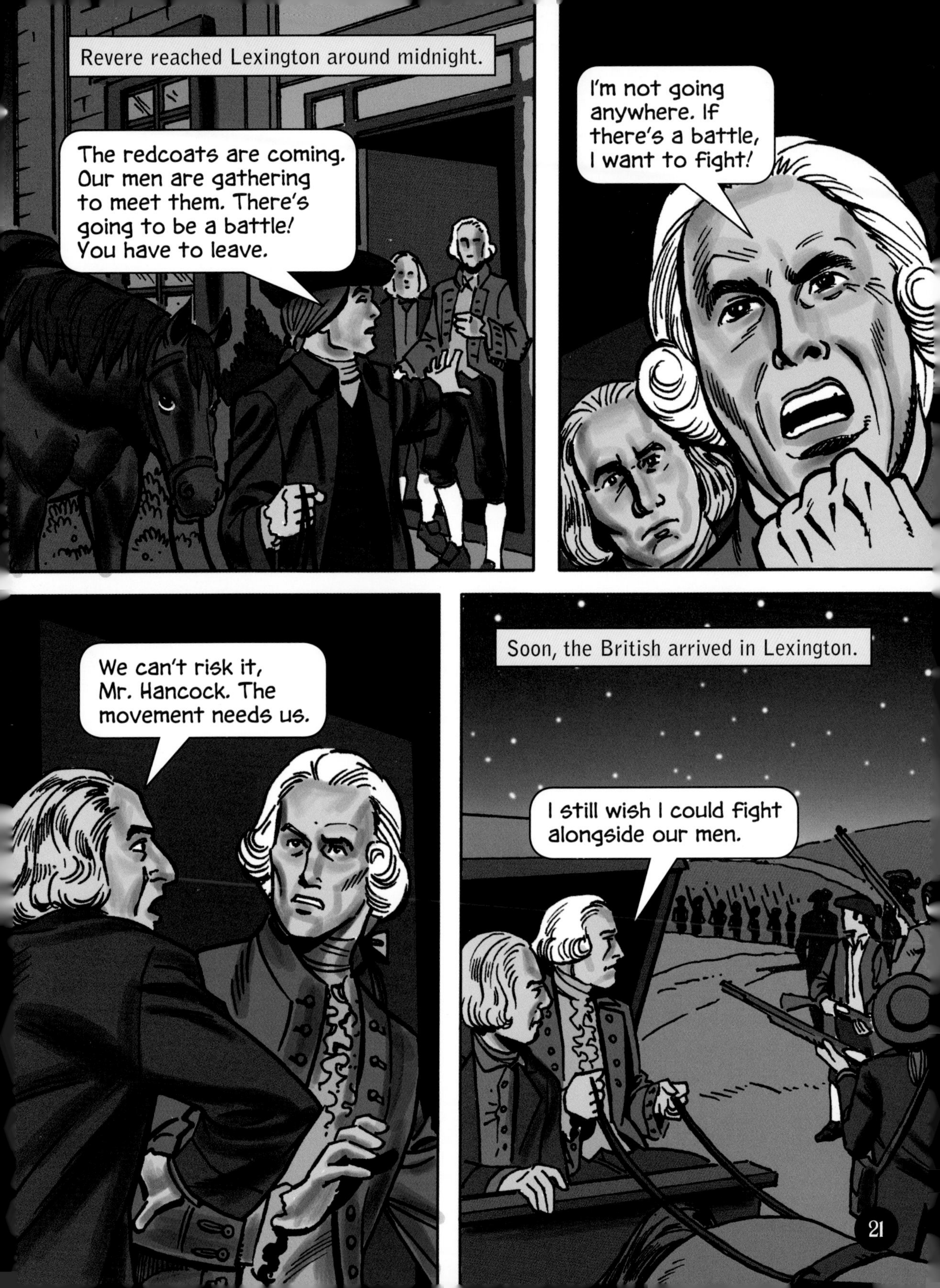
Revere reached Lexington around midnight.
The redcoats are coming. Our men are gathering to meet them. There's going to be a battle! You have to leave.
I'm not going anywhere. If there's a battle, I want to fight!
We can't risk it, Mr. Hancock. The movement needs us.
Soon, the British arrived in Lexington.
I still wish I could fight alongside our men.

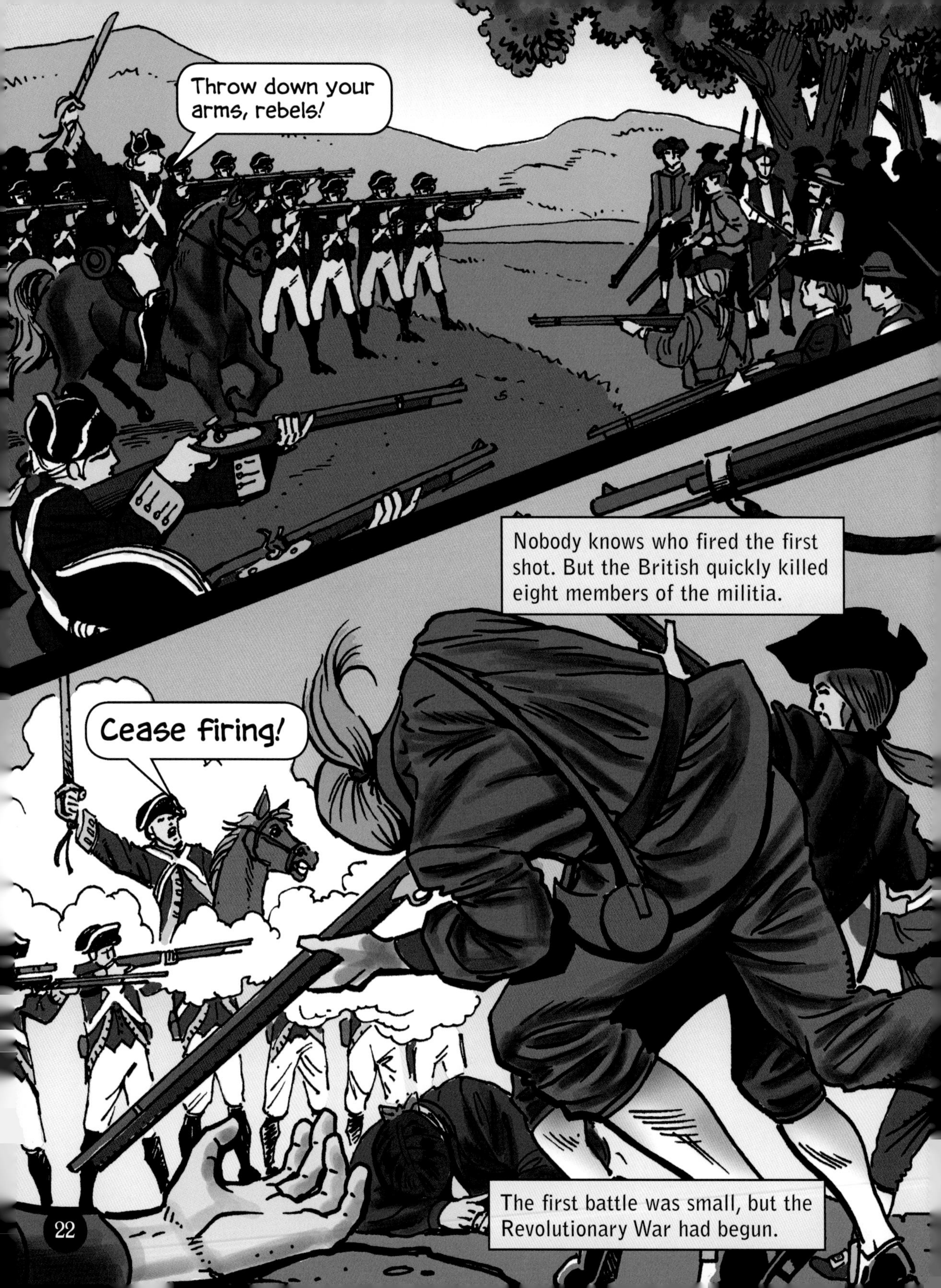
Throw down your arms, rebels!
Nobody knows who fired the first shot. But the British quickly killed eight members of the militia.
Cease firing!
The first battle was small, but the Revolutionary War had begun.

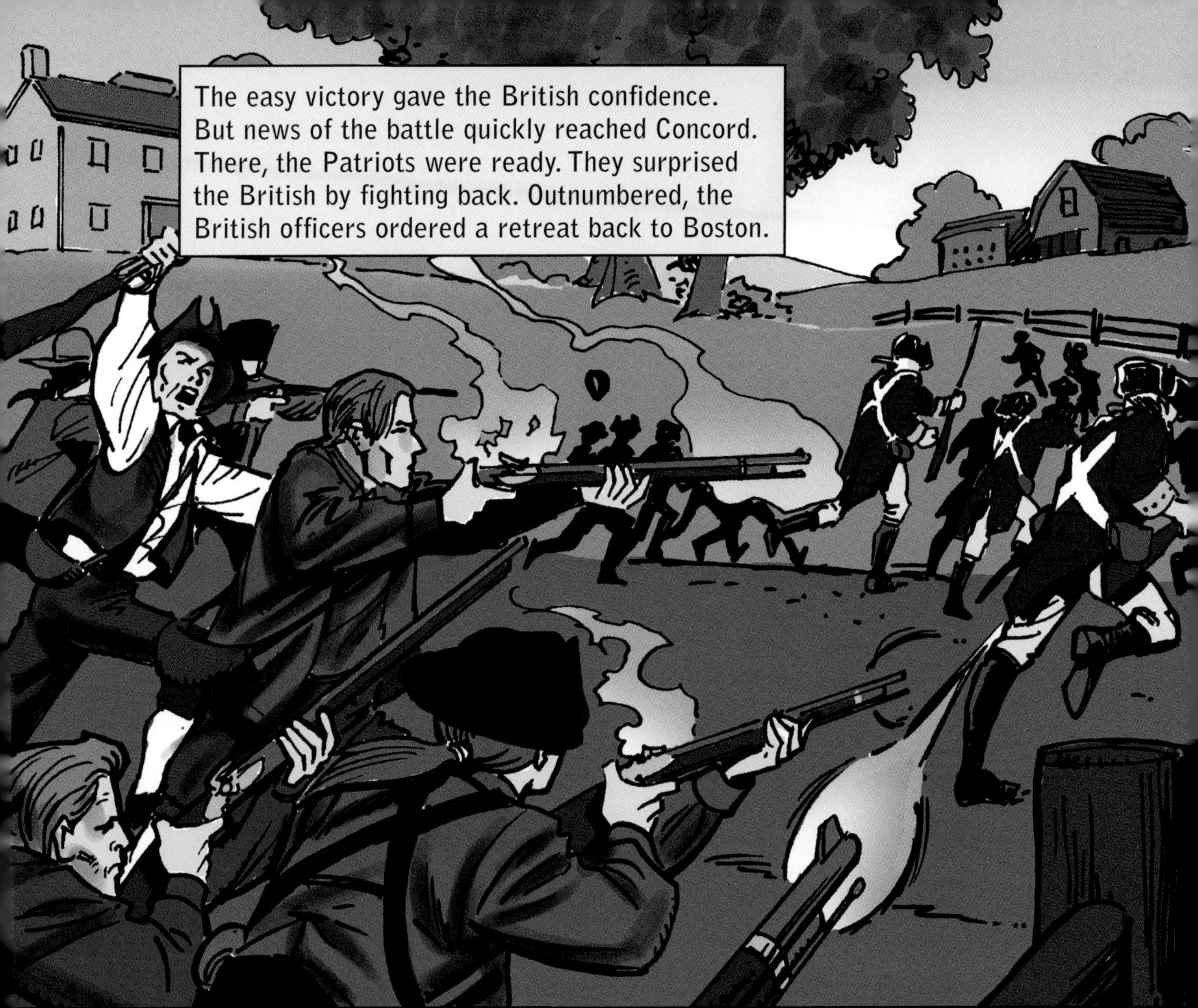
The easy victory gave the British confidence. But news of the battle quickly reached Concord. There, the Patriots were ready. They surprised the British by fighting back. Outnumbered, the British officers ordered a retreat back to Boston.

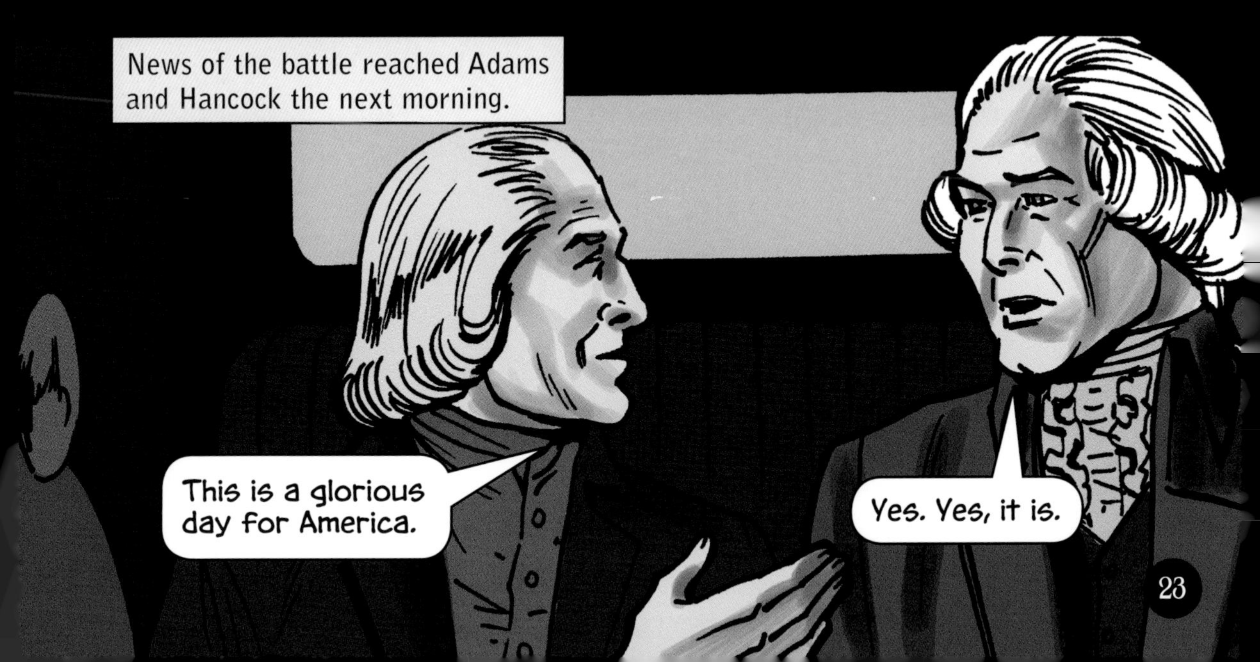
News of the battle reached Adams and Hancock the next morning.
This is a glorious day for America.
Yes. Yes, it is.

Chapter 4
A New Nation

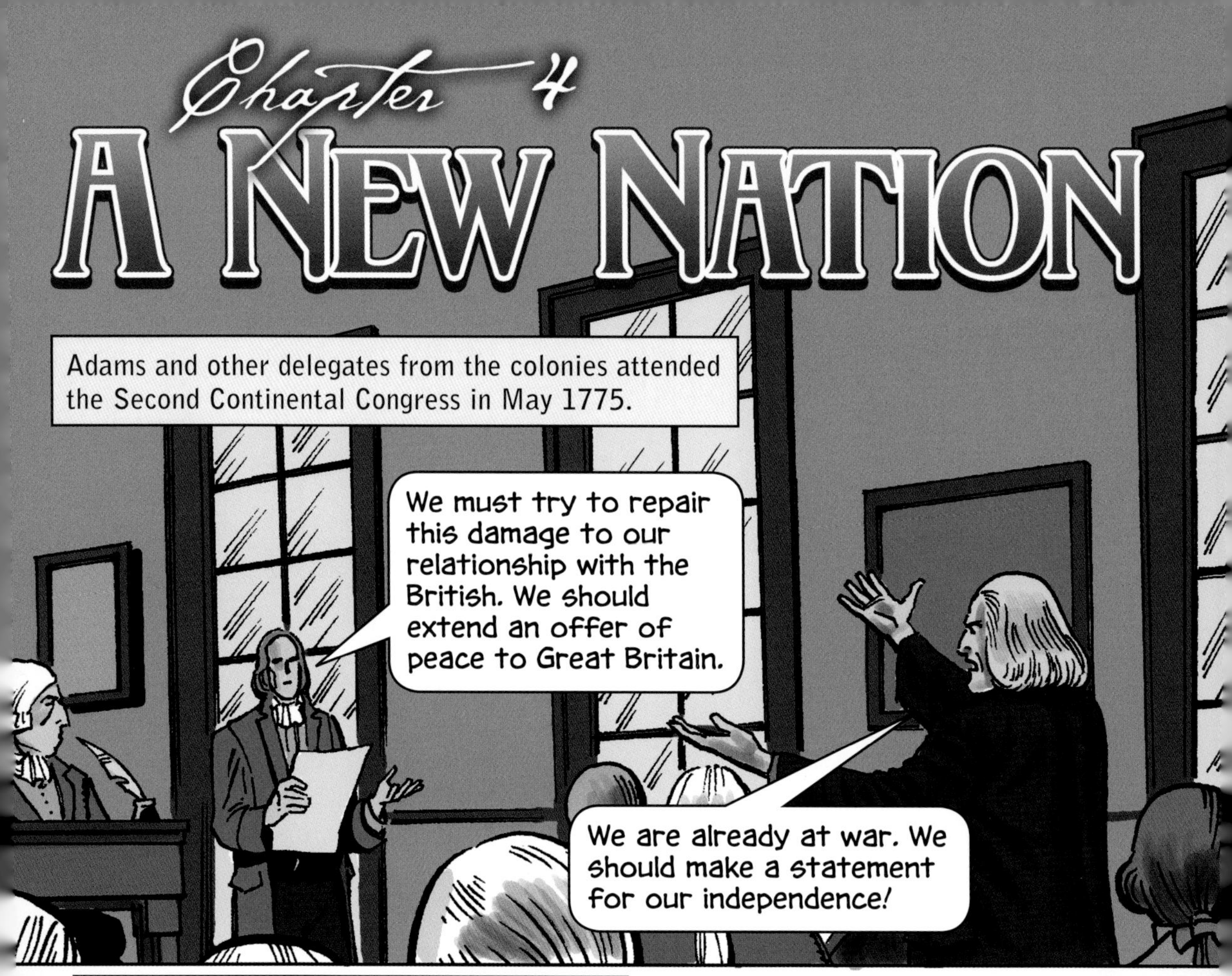

Adams and other delegates from the colonies attended the Second Continental Congress in May 1775.
We must try to repair this damage to our relationship with the British. We should extend an offer of peace to Great Britain.
We are already at war. We should make a statement for our independence!

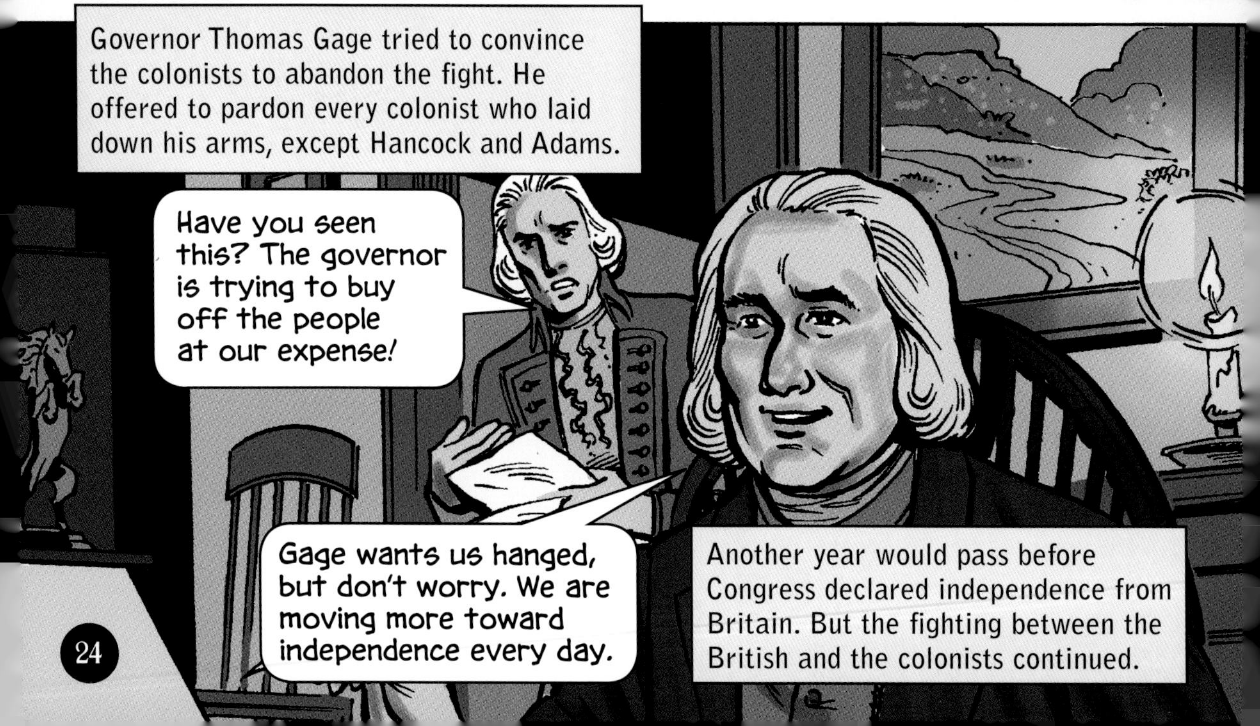

Governor Thomas Gage tried to convince the colonists to abandon the fight. He offered to pardon every colonist who laid down his arms, except Hancock and Adams.
Have you seen this? The governor is trying to buy off the people at our expense!
Gage wants us hanged, but don't worry. We are moving more toward independence every day.
Another year would pass before Congress declared independence from Britain. But the fighting between the British and the colonists continued.

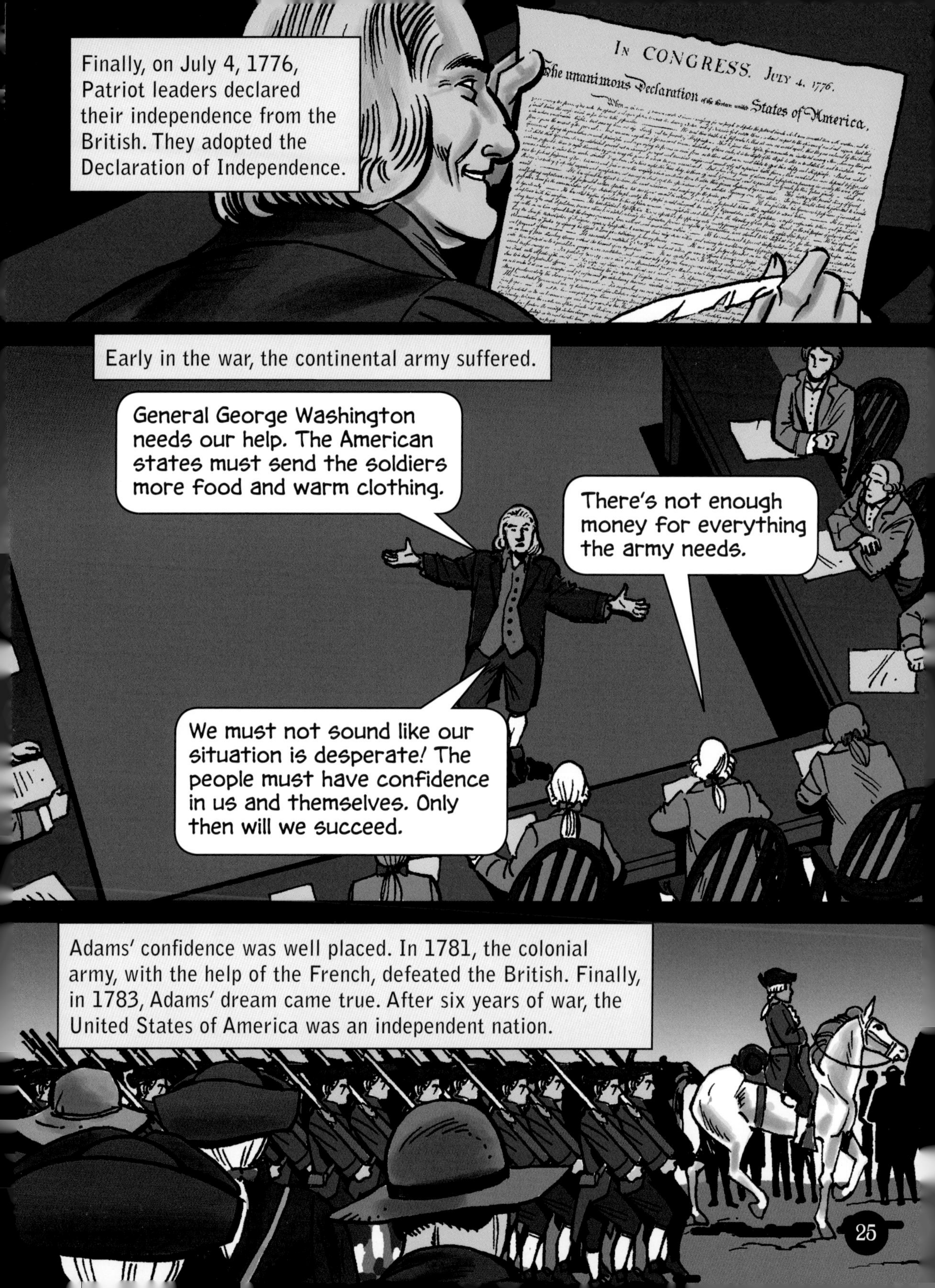
Finally, on July 4, 1776, Patriot leaders declared their independence from the British. They adopted the Declaration of Independence.
IN CONGRESS. JULY 4. 1776.
The unanimous Declaration
States of America,
Early in the war, the continental army suffered.
General George Washington needs our help. The American states must send the soldiers more food and warm clothing.
There's not enough money for everything the army needs.
We must not sound like our situation is desperate! The people must have confidence in us and themselves. Only then will we succeed.
Adams' confidence was well placed. In 1781, the colonial army, with the help of the French, defeated the British. Finally, in 1783, Adams' dream came true. After six years of war, the United States of America was an independent nation.

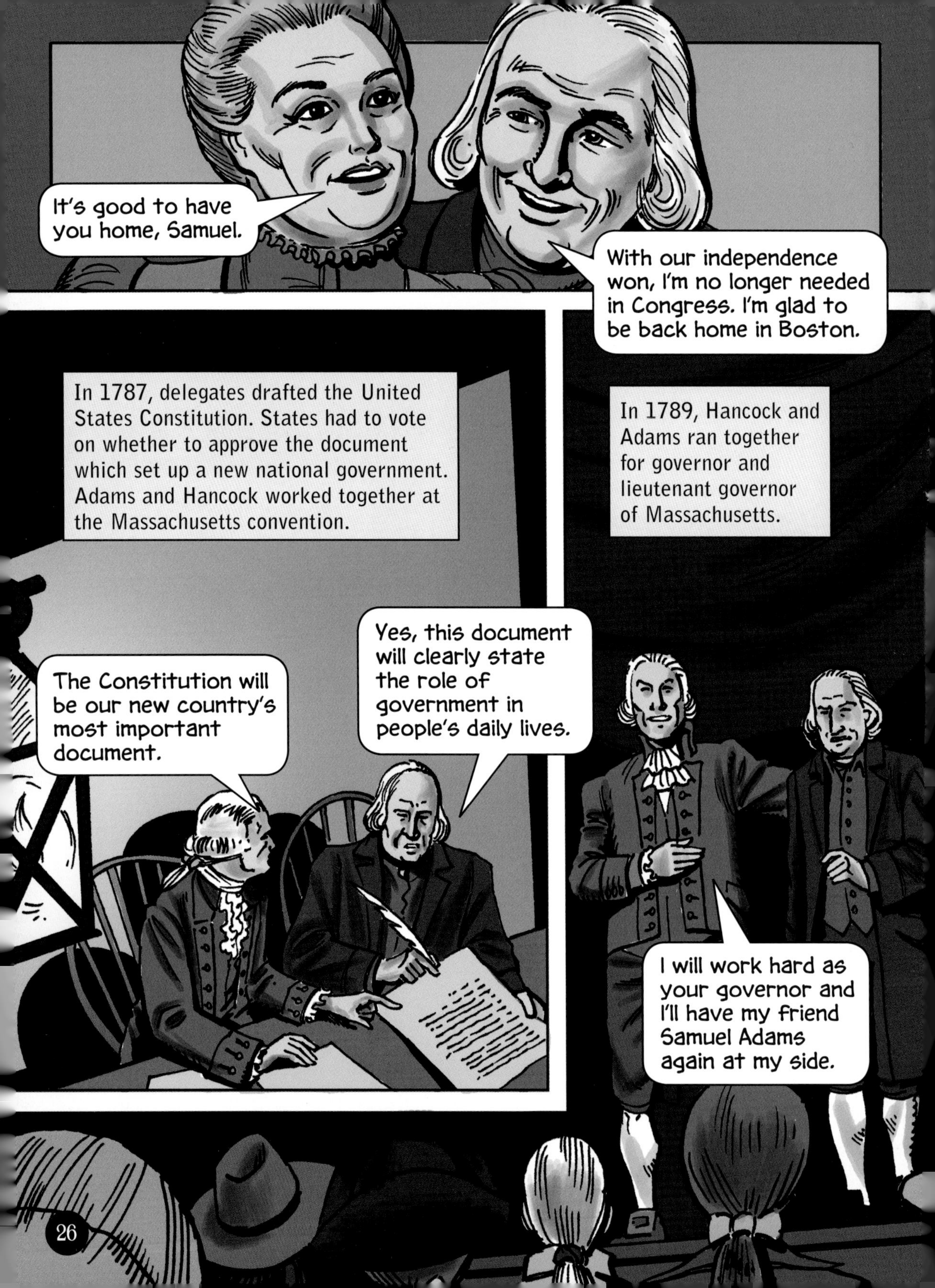
It's good to have you home, Samuel.
With our independence won, I'm no longer needed in Congress. I'm glad to be back home in Boston.
In 1787, delegates drafted the United States Constitution. States had to vote on whether to approve the document which set up a new national government. Adams and Hancock worked together at the Massachusetts convention.
The Constitution will be our new country's most important document.
Yes, this document will clearly state the role of government in people's daily lives.
In 1789, Hancock and Adams ran together for governor and lieutenant governor of Massachusetts.
I will work hard as your governor and I'll have my friend Samuel Adams again at my side.

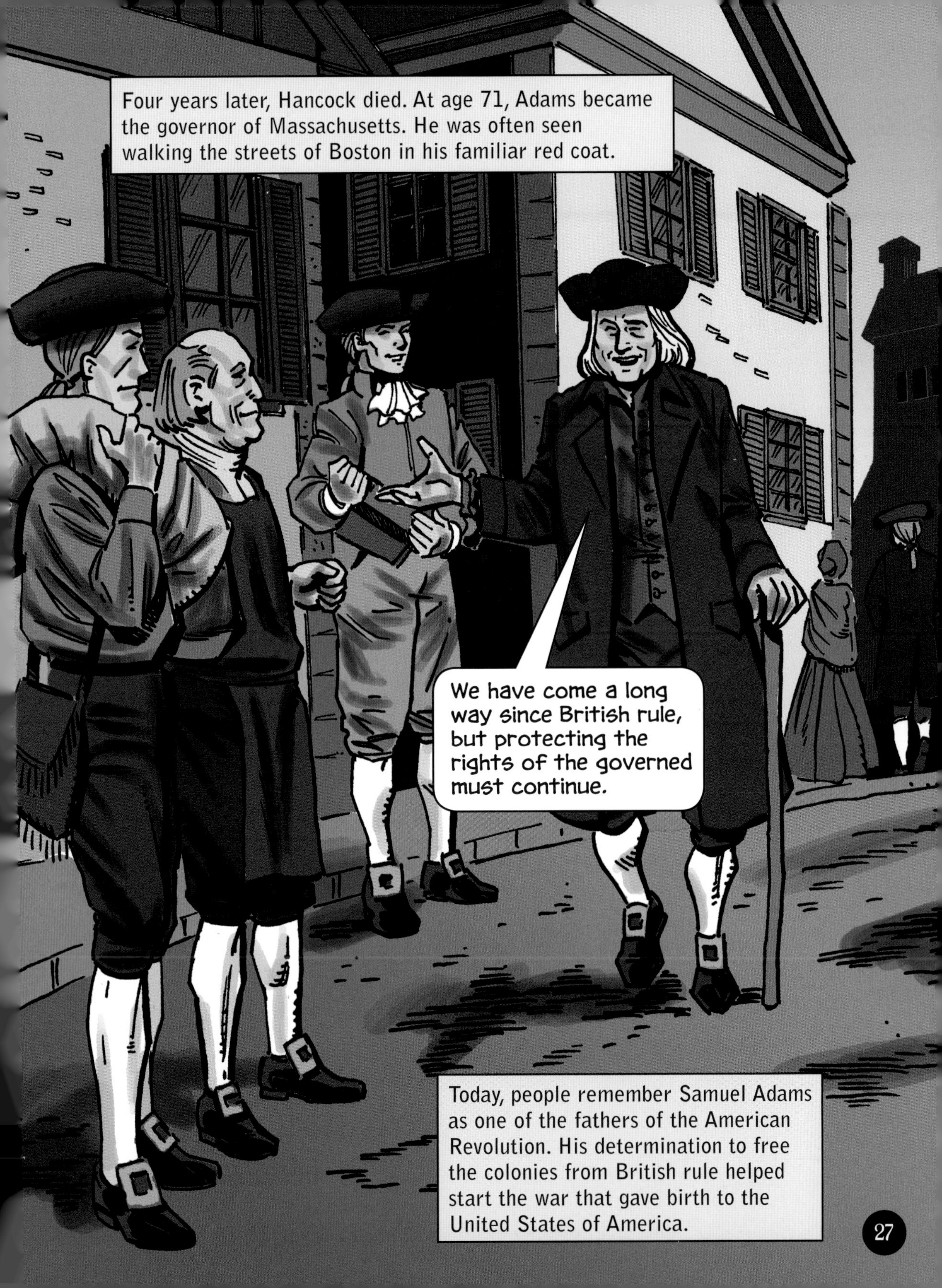
Four years later, Hancock died. At age 71, Adams became the governor of Massachusetts. He was often seen walking the streets of Boston in his familiar red coat.
We have come a long way since British rule, but protecting the rights of the governed must continue.
Today, people remember Samuel Adams as one of the fathers of the American Revolution. His determination to free the colonies from British rule helped start the war that gave birth to the United States of America.

MORE ABOUT
SAMUEL ADAMS

➤ Samuel Adams was born September 27, 1722, in Boston, Massachusetts.

➤ Even as a young man, Adams made few efforts to fit in with his peers. He refused to wear the fancy wigs that were popular for men at the time. He had little interest in fashion. He also ignored sports and riding, preferring to spend his time talking about politics. But his peers still liked him very much. He was kind and generous and was a good listener.

➤ Adams married Elizabeth Checkley in 1749. She died in 1757. In 1764, Adams married Elizabeth Wells. Adams had six children with his first wife, but only two of them, Samuel and Hannah, lived to adulthood.

➤ At around age 40, Adams developed a condition called a familial tremor. The tremor affected his movement and even his speech. His hands and head shook and his voice was often uneven because of the tremor.

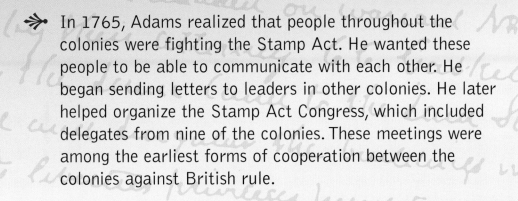

In 1765, Adams realized that people throughout the colonies were fighting the Stamp Act. He wanted these people to be able to communicate with each other. He began sending letters to leaders in other colonies. He later helped organize the Stamp Act Congress, which included delegates from nine of the colonies. These meetings were among the earliest forms of cooperation between the colonies against British rule.

John Adams, a cousin of Samuel's, went on to become the second president of the United States. But Samuel didn't agree with his cousin's politics. Instead, he sided with John Adams' political opponent, Thomas Jefferson.

At age 81, Samuel Adams died on October 2, 1803. The city of Boston honored him as a hero.

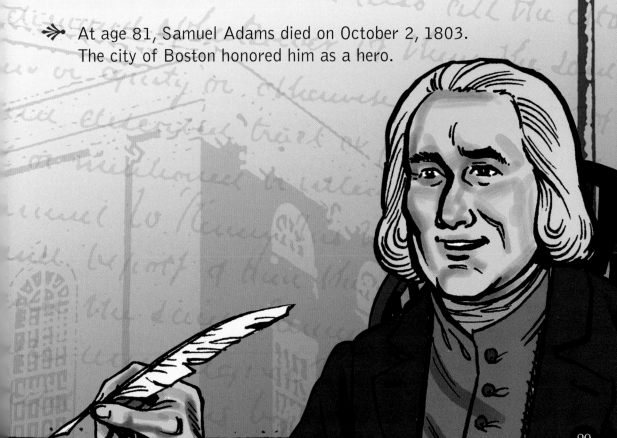

GLOSSARY

boycott (BOI-kot)—to refuse to buy certain goods as a means of protest

delegate (DEL-uh-guht)—someone who represents other people at a meeting

harbor (HAR-bur)—a place where ships load or unload their cargo

liberty (LIB-ur-tee)—freedom

massacre (MASS-uh-kur)—the brutal killing of a large number of people

militia (muh-LISH-uh)—a group of citizens who are trained to fight but only serve during an emergency

Parliament (PAR-luh-muhnt)—the governing body that makes laws for Great Britain

INTERNET SITES

FactHound offers a safe, fun way to find Internet sites related to this book. All of the sites on FactHound have been researched by our staff.

Here's how:
1. Visit *www.facthound.com*
2. Choose your grade level.
3. Type in this book ID **0736865004** for age-appropriate sites. You may also browse subjects by clicking on letters, or by clicking on pictures and words.
4. Click on the **Fetch It** button.

FactHound will fetch the best sites for you!

READ MORE

Davis, Kate. *Samuel Adams.* Triangle Histories: Revolutionary War. San Diego, Calif.: Blackbirch Press, 2002.

Doeden, Matt. *The Boston Tea Party.* Graphic Library. Mankato, Minn.: Capstone Press, 2005.

Gibson, Karen Bush. *The Life and Times of Samuel Adams.* Profiles in American History. Hockessin, Del.: Mitchell Lane, 2006.

BIBLIOGRAPHY

Adams, Samuel. *The Writings of Samuel Adams, collected and edited by Harry Alonzo Cushing.* New York: Octagon Books, 1968.

Alden, John R. *The History of the American Revolution.* New York: Knopf, 1969.

Canfield, Cass. *Samuel Adams's Revolution, 1765-1776: With the assistance of George Washington, Thomas Jefferson, Benjamin Franklin, John Adams, George III, and the People of Boston.* New York: Harper & Row, 1976.

Hosmer, James K. *Samuel Adams.* New York: Houghton Mifflin, 1899.

Miller, John C. *Sam Adams: Pioneer in Propaganda.* Boston: Little, Brown, and Company, 1936.

Zobel, Hiller B. *The Boston Massacre.* New York: W. W. Norton, 1970.

INDEX